EMPOWERFUL

ALICEA ARDITO, MSW, LCSW, MSCP

Formatted with Vellum

CONTENTS

INTRODUCTION

I'm really glad you're here. Truly.

If you're reading this, there's a good chance you want to feel better or make a change in your life, and maybe you're not entirely sure where to start. Perhaps the discomfort of staying the same has begun to outweigh the discomfort of doing something differently. Sometimes, you don't want years of processing. You want relief. You want movement. You want to feel better, *now*. And you're not alone in that.

This book mirrors the therapeutic process I've developed and used in my clinical work.

At its core is a simple belief: **meaningful change does not have to take a long time**. For many people, clarity, relief, and forward momentum happen more quickly when insight is paired with intention and action.

What *doesn't* tend to help is staying stuck in the same patterns; thinking about the same problems, telling the same stories, and hoping something will change without actually doing anything differently. Insight alone is rarely enough. Understanding why you feel the way you do is helpful, but change happens when that understanding turns into making different choices, engaging in different behaviors, and finding new ways of relating to yourself and the world.

Why I Wrote this Book

I wrote this book because I've seen this process work again and again in my psychotherapy practice.

Through education, training, and working with a wide range of clients, I've noticed something worth paying attention to: while people's stories and circumstances vary widely, the patterns that keep people stuck are often surprisingly similar.

I wanted to create something that translates what happens in therapy into a structured process that people can follow outside of the therapy space. I wanted to develop something practical and grounded. A step-by-step guide that makes the process of change feel clearer and more achievable.

This book is not a replacement for high-quality psychotherapy. In many cases, it works best alongside it. The tools and concepts you'll find here are ones many skilled therapists already use in their work. I've simply organized them into a clear, structured process you can apply in your daily life.

What This Book Is - and What it Isn't

Setting expectations is part of building trust.

This book offers a therapeutic method designed to help you better understand yourself, clarify what's important to you, and begin making changes that move your life in a direction that feels more aligned and meaningful. It supports personal growth, life transitions, self-reflection, and behavioral change. It may be especially helpful if you feel stuck, if you've tried to make changes before without success, or if you feel ready to move forward but want a clearer path.

However, this book is not a magic wand. Reading it alone will not create change. The work belongs to you. My role here is similar to what I do with clients: to provide structure, psychoeducation, reflective questions, and guidance that helps facilitate your process. The insight, the effort, and the action ultimately come from you.

There are also limits to what this book can do for you. It is not intended to treat severe mental health conditions or replace professional care. If you are experiencing a mental health crisis - such as thoughts of harming yourself, feeling unsafe, or losing touch with reality - it's critical to seek immediate support from a qualified professional or crisis service. In the United States, you can call or text 988 for immediate help.

Please also remember that you do not have to be in immediate danger to seek professional help. Support from a qualified mental health professional can be valuable long before a situation reaches the level of crisis.

A Multidirectional Approach to Change

My approach looks at change from multiple directions. What I mean by that is that we will explore the past, present, and future. We look back to understand what happened and why. We assess present circumstances, including current stressors, habits, beliefs, and barriers. Then we look forward intentionally, toward the kind of life you want to be living. When someone spends too much time focused only on the past, it can become difficult to imagine a different future. Without direction, action stalls. Insight needs forward movement to become meaningful change.

This book will guide you through a process that changes both thinking and behavior. In *Part I: Assess,* I will help you to clearly see where you are physically, socially and personally, without judgment or overwhelm. Next in *Part II: Align,* you will explore your inner world, which consists of your values, beliefs and thoughts, so that your choices and actions will reflect your authentic self. And finally, in *Part III: Activate,* you will turn your clarity into action, build momentum through behavior, and develop resilience that sustains change over time.

The order is intentional. Many people will want to jump directly into action, especially if they have been feeling stuck. But taking action without having clarity and alignment often leads to frustration or short-lived change. By moving through these parts in sequence, your actions will be more intentional, sustainable, and meaningful.

How to Use this Book

This book is designed to be approached as a process. I encourage you to read the chapters in order rather than skipping ahead. And I say this as a person who will often skip to the last chapter or last page just to find out the ending! The structure reflects the same sequence I use when working with clients, which developed over years of clinical experience. Each section builds on the previous one, introducing concepts in a logical way, which ultimately prepares you for meaningful change.

Move through the book at your own pace. Pause when something resonates. Spend time reflecting on the questions and exercises. You may find that certain sections invite you to slow down, or may necessitate rereading the ideas presented more than once. My hope is that there are clear takeaways for you in each section.

Consider Keeping a Journal

Many readers will find it helpful to keep a journal while moving through this process. Over time, you will begin creating your own roadmap, which you can revisit, revise, and learn from as you continue moving through the *Empowerful* framework.

There is no single "right" way to do this. We do not all think the same, thankfully. Some of you may write in narrative form, exploring your thoughts and feelings in paragraphs. Others might prefer bullet points, lists, or checkboxes. Some readers may respond directly to the reflection questions at the end of each chapter, while others may use them simply as prompts for their own ideas. Perhaps you write a thousand words, or a single sentence.

You might draw, sketch, and use color to capture your thoughts visually. You might write poetry. You might jot down a few simple observations. Perhaps you use technology to capture your thoughts. However you choose to record your reflections is the right way for you. Please approach this process in a way that feels natural and authentic to **you.**

What You Can Expect

Here's what you can expect:

- A clear framework to understand where you are
- Tools to align your values, beliefs, and choices
- Practical strategies to take action — even when motivation is low
- Support for navigating setbacks without judgment or shame

You don't need endless effort to feel better. You don't need to become someone you're not. You need a process that honors your reality and helps you move forward.

My hope is that you finish this book feeling empowered and powerful.

Empowerful.

PART I

ASSESS

Your Body • Your World • Your Capacity

People come to see me for many reasons. Relationships. Life transitions. Difficult thoughts. Grief. Anxiety. Low mood. Trouble focusing. Sometimes all of the above, at once. And almost everyone who walks into my office has one thing in common: **they want to feel better.**

More specifically, they often want to *do something* that will help them to feel better. Anything, really. Because when you feel uncomfortable, overwhelmed, or frustrated, action can feel like relief. Doing something is better than doing nothing. Right?

Not always.

As a society we are often taught that problems should be solved quickly. Something is wrong, so fix it. The dumpster is on fire, so put it out. Fair enough. But what caused the blaze in the first place?

That's why Assess comes first.

When therapy starts, most people want to dive right in. They want to unload everything that's been swirling in their head: the thoughts they haven't said out loud, the feelings they've been dealing with, the chaos they've been trying to manage. For many people, the therapy room is the first place they've felt safe enough to say what has been taking up space in their mind. Sometimes it's the first chance they've had to slow down long enough to think clearly and start putting the pieces together.

As a social worker, I'm trained to meet people where they are. So that's what I do first. I begin where my client needs to start. I allow space to vent, to explore, to get it all out. And then we slow down, because if we move too fast, we risk missing something vital. That's where assessment comes in.

When a client is skeptical or impatient, I explain why assessment matters. We can use cognitive-behavioral strategies, motivational interviewing, emotionally focused work - all kinds of interventions - but if the root of someone's anxiety, low mood, or irritability is physiological, environmental, or situational, then we're working hard on the wrong problem, or using the wrong approach.

That's what happens when you rush into action before you really understand what's going on. You can end up trying to fix something that isn't actually broken, while missing the thing that needs your attention most. I've had countless clients come in convinced they already knew what the problem was, only to find that the picture looked very different once we slowed down and looked at all of it.

Assessment means slowing down and gathering information before choosing solutions.

Imagine someone who comes into therapy saying they feel constantly anxious and unable to concentrate at work. It would be easy to jump straight into anxiety-management tools or productivity strategies. But assessment asks us to pause and look deeper. How has their sleep been? What does their routine look like? Are they living on caffeine? Have there been recent stressors? Could there be a medical issue? Is their work environment unusually demanding, unstable, or just plain unsustainable?

Sometimes the answer is somewhere people didn't initially think to look. I've seen "anxiety" turn out to be sleep deprivation, untreated ADHD, thyroid issues, chronic stress, or a work environment that would make almost anyone feel terrible. Once the full picture becomes clearer, the path forward usually starts to make more sense.

There's an important distinction here: **assessing yourself is not the same as judging yourself.**

That difference takes intention and practice.

Some people approach assessment through a perfectionistic lens, where every difficulty feels like failure. Others, especially those with trauma histories, may interpret struggle as proof that they're broken. Some feel overwhelmed by the idea that they might be part of the problem at all. Every one of these responses deserves compassion rather than criticism.

From a social work perspective, we use a framework called *person-in-environment*. It's foundational. People do not exist in a vacuum. We are shaped by biological, psychological, social, and spiritual influences. From the moment we are born, our experiences, relationships, expectations, and environments begin shaping how we cope, relate, and survive.

Because of that, understanding yourself often means trying to organize and make sense of those experiences. There is value in naming symptoms and giving certain clusters of experience a label. Clinical diagnoses can be useful. They can guide treatment and provide clarity. But when someone begins to see themselves as nothing more than a diagnosis or a list of symptoms, the wider context gets lost.

For example, imagine two people who both report feeling chronically exhausted and irritable. One is working a demanding job, caring for aging parents, and sleeping five hours a night. The other is experiencing untreated depression after a major life loss. On the surface, the symptoms may look similar, but the context is not. And context is worth paying attention to, because it helps determine what kind of support might actually help.

This is why assessment is essential. When we step back and look at the full picture of a person's life, patterns start to emerge.

And yes, sometimes that process increases discomfort before it brings relief. That makes sense. You're unpacking. I normalize this with clients all the time. Sometimes you do feel worse before you feel better. But once things begin to make sense, relief often follows.

I often use a jigsaw puzzle analogy.

Therapy helps identify the pieces and then supports you as you put them together. Anyone who has ever opened a thousand-piece puzzle knows that moment of overwhelm after dumping everything onto the table. Pieces everywhere, no obvious starting point, no clear order. You might begin with the corners. Maybe the straight edges. Maybe one small recognizable pattern. Sometimes you don't even know what the final picture looks like yet. That's okay.

Therapy works this way.

And so does the *Empowerful* method.

1

YOUR BODY

Your body has been talking to you your entire life. Many of us simply didn't learn how to listen to it.

We have been taught to disconnect from our bodies. We learn to ignore signs and symptoms, push past what the body is telling us, and override its needs in the name of doing better, being better, performing better, and looking better.

A lot of people learn to treat their body like a project, an obstacle, or a machine. Something that needs to look a certain way in order to be acceptable. Something that should perform on demand. In that mindset, fatigue becomes laziness. Hunger becomes lack of discipline. Stress gets reframed as ambition. Pain becomes something to push through so you don't look weak. Rest becomes something you earn only after everything else is done.

Over time, that messaging can make basic care feel optional, indulgent, or even shameful.

And this disconnection is reinforced all around us.

We live in a productivity culture that rewards override. Parts of the wellness industry profit from keeping people dissatisfied, hypervigilant, or convinced that they are only one habit away from finally becoming acceptable. When you are taught to listen to those messages instead of trusting your body, you become easier to influence, and frankly, easier to sell to.

There are other social forces shaping this too. Many men are socialized to equate stoicism with strength, which can make it harder to acknowledge pain, exhaustion, stress, or the need for help. Many women are socialized to minimize their needs, stay pleasant and productive, and tolerate having symptoms dismissed or explained away. Race, class, living with disability, caregiving demands, chronic illness, trauma, and access to care play a role here as well. Advice such as "sleep more," "eat better," or "just take care of yourself" lands very differently depending on the conditions someone is actually living within.

So before this chapter asks you to pay attention to your body, I want to be very clear about something. This chapter is not a moral inventory. It is not a performance review. It is not another opportunity to blame yourself for being human. It is an invitation to get honest about what your body has been carrying, and what it might be trying to tell you.

To do that, it helps to understand something fundamental: you experience life in a physical body. One you didn't get to custom-order ahead of time!

Your energy, focus, mood, and resilience are shaped by physical systems working together every day. Sleep, nutrition, movement, stress, and overall health influence how you feel. When these systems are supported, life often feels more manageable. When they're strained, even simple things can feel heavier. Motivation may fade. Focus can slip. Emotional regulation takes more effort. This is simply how the body responds when it's being pushed beyond what it can comfortably handle.

Your body has been giving you information all along through energy levels, cravings, tension, restlessness, mood shifts, pain, and fatigue. These signals are not problems to eliminate or obstacles to overcome. They provide information. They tell you what your body needs and how it's responding to your environment.

The goal here is to notice these signals with curiosity and start exploring what they may be telling you.

Why We Begin With the Physical Body

We begin with the physical body because it is foundational. Your physiology directly influences how you feel, think, and function.

Many physical health conditions can produce or intensify mental health symptoms, sometimes making them appear primarily psychological at first. In some cases, emotional distress is less about faulty thinking and more to do with a body that is struggling to regulate itself.

There are medical and physiological conditions that present with symptoms like low mood, anxiety, irritability, or brain fog, even though the root cause is physical. Without awareness of this connection, people can spend years trying to "think" their way out of symptoms that require physical attention.

This is a key reason to assess the physical body.

In my clinical work, I've seen this play out many times. A client may come in reporting low energy, low motivation, and persistent low mood. They genuinely want to make changes in their life, yet progress feels stalled despite insight and effort. When this happens, it's worth pausing to ask whether something else might be contributing, whether the barrier is less psychological and more physiological.

I remember one client who became increasingly frustrated with herself because she couldn't focus the way she used to. She described feeling like she couldn't retain information and struggled to stay engaged with tasks that required concentration. Things that had once felt simple now took significantly more effort, and she began to question her ability to keep up at work. She started to wonder if this was a problem with her motivation or discipline.

As we explored further, she mentioned a fall a few months earlier. At the time, she hadn't thought much of it. There was no formal diagnosis, and she had moved on quickly. But the timing lined up. With some follow-up and medical evaluation, it became clear that her symptoms were consistent with a mild concussion. What she had been trying to push through was actually her brain recovering from an injury.

Sometimes this exploration includes ruling out underlying medical concerns through routine care. Other times, it reveals something more basic and easier to overlook. For example, a client once realized they were routinely going most of the day without eating. By early afternoon, they were exhausted, foggy, and discouraged, and interpreting these symptoms as a lack of motivation or willpower. In reality, there was simply no fuel in the tank.

With small, supportive changes, such as adding a protein-rich breakfast and light exercise in the morning, their energy began to improve within weeks. That increased capacity made it possible to engage more fully in the rest of the therapeutic work. Once basic needs were supported, other changes no longer felt quite so out of reach.

This isn't meant to suggest that a simple adjustment will be the solution for everyone. It's not about offering false hope or quick fixes. It's about recognizing that when foundational needs aren't being met, even the best psychological work can stall. When the body is supported, capacity often increases, along with the ability to make meaningful change.

When Physical Conditions Mimic Mental Health Symptoms

The brain and body are not separate systems. They are deeply interconnected. The brain is a physical organ, and like every other organ in the body, it responds to changes in hormones, inflammation, blood sugar, sleep quality, oxygen levels, and many other physiological processes. When those systems are strained or out of balance, the brain can respond with symptoms that feel emotional or psychological, such as anxiety, low mood, irritability, difficulty concentrating, or mental fatigue.

If your mood, focus, or emotional regulation feel off, your brain may be part of the picture, and that is completely normal. The brain is constantly interpreting signals from the body and the environment and trying to keep everything in balance. Sometimes what feels like a psychological struggle is actually the brain responding to physiological stress, illness, nutritional deficiencies, sleep disruption, or hormonal shifts.

In my clinical experience, this shows up in very practical ways. A common example is low energy. Many clients arrive convinced that fatigue must mean depression or lack of motivation. And sometimes it does. But there are many other possibilities. Low energy can be a result of cumulative stress, poor nutrition, sleep disruption, hormonal changes, medication side effects, or underlying medical issues. The body may simply be depleted.

Anxiety is another good example. People often assume it begins with a thought or emotional trigger, but that is not always the case. Anxiety can be influenced by medication side effects, shifts in hormones such as cortisol or adrenaline, changes in the menstrual cycle, or fluctuations in blood sugar related to diet. When the body is physiologically activated, the brain interprets those signals and tries to make sense of them.

When I explain the brain–body connection to clients, I often use a simple analogy. Your pancreas is an organ. Your lungs are an organ. Your brain is an organ, too. These organs do not function independently of one another. They are part of interconnected systems that are constantly communicating. The brain does not exist separately from the rest of the body. Even though we sometimes experience ourselves as what one client described as "a thinking mind inside a body," the physical systems underneath are always interacting.

Sometimes it can be difficult to tell which signal came first. Did the brain respond to something happening in the body, or did the body respond to something happening in the mind? It can feel a bit like the chicken-and-egg question.

Consider a moment of panic. A person might feel sweaty, their heart begins to race, their chest tightens, and they feel lightheaded. Did the panic begin with a frightening thought or external stressor that triggered the body's response? Or did the body experience a small physiological shift, maybe a change in heart rate or a sensation of dizziness, and the brain interpreted that signal as danger, which then escalated into panic? Sometimes it isn't immediately clear. Part of the work of assessment is exploring these patterns with curiosity.

How This Shows Up in the Body

You may be surprised by how many common medical conditions can contribute to symptoms that look like mental health concerns. Below are examples grouped by body system. The goal here is to show how interconnected the body and mind really are.

Endocrine / Hormonal Conditions

- **Hyperthyroidism** → anxiety, panic, irritability, insomnia.
- **Hypothyroidism** → depression, fatigue, cognitive slowing.
- **Perimenopause/menopause** → mood swings, anxiety, depression.
- **Low testosterone** → depression, low motivation, irritability.
- **Cushing's syndrome** → depression, anxiety, emotional lability.

Neurological Conditions

- **Traumatic brain injury (TBI)** → mood changes, impulsivity, depression, anxiety.
- **Epilepsy** → anxiety, depression, dissociation-like symptoms.
- **Parkinson's disease** → depression, apathy, anxiety.

- **Multiple sclerosis (MS)** → depression, cognitive changes, emotional regulation difficulties.

Cardiovascular & Respiratory Conditions

- **Heart rhythm disorders** → anxiety or panic-like symptoms.
- **Asthma / COPD** → anxiety related to breathlessness.
- **Postural Orthostatic Tachycardia Syndrome (POTS)** → anxiety, brain fog, panic-like symptoms.

Metabolic & Nutritional Issues

- **Vitamin B12 deficiency** → depression, irritability, cognitive changes.
- **Iron-deficiency anemia** → fatigue, depression, anxiety.
- **Blood sugar dysregulation** (diabetes, hypoglycemia) → mood swings, anxiety, irritability.

Autoimmune & Inflammatory Conditions

- **Lupus** → depression, anxiety, cognitive changes.
- **Rheumatoid arthritis** → depression related to inflammation and chronic pain.
- **Hashimoto's thyroiditis** → depression, anxiety, brain fog.

Sleep-Related Conditions

- **Sleep apnea** → depression, irritability, anxiety, cognitive impairment.
- **Chronic insomnia** → anxiety, mood instability, concentration difficulties.

Infectious or Post-Viral Conditions

- **Long COVID** → anxiety, depression, brain fog.
- **Lyme disease** → mood changes, anxiety, cognitive symptoms.

Substance- or Medication-Related Effects

- **Steroids (e.g., prednisone)** → mood swings, anxiety, agitation.
- **Stimulants** → anxiety, insomnia.
- **Alcohol use** → depression and anxiety, particularly during withdrawal.

Medication Effects and Side Effects: An Often Overlooked Variable

This is where I get to use the last four letters behind my name, my MSCP.

My education in clinical psychopharmacology has been a meaningful complement to my work as a clinical social worker, largely because many of the people I work with take medication, have taken medication in the past, or are considering it now.

Medication effects and side effects are a key and often overlooked factor when considering mood, energy, anxiety, focus, and emotional regulation.

Medication decisions are deeply personal and always involve weighing potential benefits alongside possible risks and side effects. For many people, medication is life-changing and essential. For others, side effects can be significant, sometimes outweighing the original symptoms or introducing new ones that feel unmanageable or even intolerable.

Side effects are real. Some are common and well-documented. Others are rare. Some show up immediately; others emerge gradually over time. And while dosing guidelines are standardized, people are not. Medications can affect individuals differently based on body composition, metabolism, age, hormonal status, genetics, and overall health.

It's also worth keeping in mind that medications are developed and tested under controlled conditions that don't fully reflect the complexity of real life. Clinical trials are designed to isolate the effects of a medication, which often means limiting who can participate. People with multiple medical conditions, those taking several medications, pregnant individuals, children and adolescents, and older adults are often excluded in early stages of research.

Historically, women, certain racial and ethnic populations, and individuals with diverse body types have also been underrepresented in clinical trials. As a result, the populations studied do not always reflect the wide range of people who will eventually take these medications in real-world settings.

When medications move into everyday use, they are taken by people with diverse genetic backgrounds, hormonal patterns, metabolic rates, health histories, and environmental stressors. Those differences influence how medications are absorbed, metabolized, and experienced in the body, which is why real-world responses don't always match textbook expectations.

In my clinical work, one of the most common misunderstandings I see about psychiatric medication is the belief that it is one-size-fits-all. That assumption simply isn't accurate. Not everyone will experience a medication in the same way, even when they share a diagnosis or are prescribed the same dosage.

I've worked with clients who felt blindsided by symptoms that didn't respond to their usual coping strategies. It wasn't because those strategies stopped working, it was because something physiological had shifted.

One client with a long history of thyroid dysfunction experienced a sudden increase in anxiety that felt unfamiliar and unmanageable. There was no clear trigger, and the tools that typically helped weren't touching it. When we slowed down and revisited the timeline, we realized her thyroid medication dosage had been adjusted several weeks earlier. The anxiety was a side effect. Once the dosage was reassessed, her symptoms settled.

Another client experienced increasing distress in her relationship because sex had become unsatisfying and began to feel like a chore, creating tension with her spouse. She believed this was an inevitable consequence of neuropathy and assumed nothing could be done. When we looked more closely, the onset of these changes lined up with starting a medication for neuropathic pain. One of its known side effects, which had never been explained to her, was reduced sexual desire and difficulty achieving orgasm. She hadn't raised the concern with her physician, partly because she was private and partly because she didn't know there could be a connection. After tapering off that medication and trying an alternative without the same side-effect profile, the issue resolved.

I want to be clear that I am not for or against medication as a general rule. Medication decisions are incredibly personal and should involve careful consideration of potential benefits, risks, and side effects. My role is to support clients who are considering medication by helping them feel informed, empowered to ask questions, and able to make decisions that feel right for them.

That includes understanding how long a medication may take to work, how it might be discontinued in the future, whether it is intended for short-term or longer-term use, and what other treatment options may exist. It also includes discussing possible side effects openly.

For example, some commonly prescribed medications for depression may carry metabolic side effects that can contribute to weight gain. For some people that may feel manageable; for others it may be unacceptable. Other medications may affect sexual functioning, including decreased desire or difficulty achieving orgasm. For some individuals this may not be a significant concern, while for others, it may be a dealbreaker.

Preferences like these shape informed consent. Informed consent means understanding the potential outcomes and deciding which trade-offs feel acceptable to you.

Ultimately, medication decisions should be collaborative. Providers bring medical training and expertise, and you bring the lived experience of your body. When those two perspectives work together, care becomes more thoughtful, individualized, and effective.

A Note on Advocacy

Talking with medical providers about side effects or concerns can feel intimidating, and there are many reasons for that.

Healthcare settings often involve an inherent power difference between provider and patient. The provider has specialized knowledge, authority, and limited time, while the patient may feel vulnerable, uncertain, or worried about being perceived as difficult. Many people also feel rushed during appointments, either by the provider or their own awareness that time is limited.

Social dynamics can make this even more complicated. Some people have experienced having their symptoms minimized or dismissed in the past. Women, in particular, have historically had their symptoms taken less seriously in medical settings. For others, conversations may quickly shift toward weight regardless of the concern being presented. Race, gender identity, sexual orientation, disability, and socioeconomic status can also shape how comfortable or safe someone feels speaking up in medical environments. When multiple factors intersect, the experience can become even more complicated.

There are also practical realities in healthcare systems today. Some providers are working under intense time pressure and administrative demands. Others may have different communication styles. Many are compassionate professionals who genuinely want to help, but the structure of the system can still make conversations feel rushed or one-sided.

All of this means that speaking up about side effects or concerns can require more effort than it should. Many people worry about sounding dramatic, difficult, or ungrateful for treatment. But asking questions and sharing what you're experiencing is part of good medical care. Describing what has changed, when it changed, and how it is affecting your life provides essential information that helps ensure you and your provider are working on the right problem.

Advocating for Yourself in Medical Conversations (Without Feeling Dramatic or Dismissed)

Many people hesitate to bring up side effects with medical providers. They worry about sounding dramatic, difficult, ungrateful, or like they're "complaining". (Medical gaslighting is real, by the way!) Some people assume they should tolerate discomfort if a medication is technically working. Others don't realize that what they're experiencing could even be related.

Here's the truth. Reporting side effects isn't you being dramatic. It is clinically relevant information that helps guide your care.

Your provider can only work with what they know: mood changes, anxiety, fatigue, sleep disruption, sexual side effects, brain fog, or emotional blunting are not minor details. They directly affect quality of life, relationships, and daily functioning. You are not expected to endure them.

If it helps, approach the conversation with neutral, observable language rather than self-judgment or apology.

For example:

- "I've noticed an increase in anxiety since this dose was adjusted."
- "These symptoms started about three weeks after beginning this medication."
- "Something feels different in my body, and I want to make sure we're not missing a connection."

- "The medication is helping in some ways, but the side effects are impacting my day-to-day life."

You don't need to prove anything. You don't need the "perfect" explanation. Your observations alone are valuable data.

It's also reasonable to ask questions such as:

- "Is this a known side effect?"
- "Are there alternative options with a different side effect profile?"
- "What would we expect if this were medication-related?"

If a concern is minimized or dismissed, that does not mean your experience isn't real. It may mean the conversation needs to continue, or that another provider's perspective could be helpful. You are the expert on your lived experience. Providers bring medical education and training. You bring the data of your body. Care becomes more effective with collaboration, and seeking clarity is a form of self-advocacy.

If something in your body is off, it will influence how you feel, think, and function. That's because the mind and body are connected, and what affects one usually affects the other. Once we've considered medical factors and medication effects, the next step is to look at the other physiological processes that shape how you think, feel, and function every day.

Your job here is to stay curious. This is a thorough assessment, and you're gathering information that can give you greater insight and clarity as you move through the Empowerful process. From here, we start looking at the things your body interacts with every day: the food that fuels you, the hydration that keeps your body functioning well, the movement that supports your health, the sleep that restores you, and the ways you respond to your environment.

This is where things start to get practical.

Food as Fuel for Energy and Stability

Food is one of the most frequent and influential inputs into your body. What you eat, and how consistently you eat, plays a significant role in your energy level, mood, focus, stress response, and overall sense of well-being.

Your brain relies on a steady supply of nutrients to function effectively, including regulating mood, attention, and emotional balance. Neurotransmitters such as serotonin, dopamine, and norepinephrine, which influence motivation, calmness, and focus, are built from nutrients found in food.

When meals are skipped, overly restrictive, or significantly imbalanced, blood sugar levels can fluctuate, and mood often shifts as a result. This can show up as irritability, anxiety, low mood, difficulty concentrating, or increased emotional reactivity. These responses are physiological.

Energy isn't just about how much you eat. It's also about consistency and balance. When meals are heavily weighted toward refined carbohydrates or sugar without enough protein, fiber, or fat, energy levels often spike and then crash. These swings can show up as midday fatigue, brain fog, increased cravings, or a growing reliance on caffeine or sugar for quick relief.

Balanced meals tend to support steadier energy throughout the day by slowing digestion, stabilizing blood sugar, and providing sustained fuel to the brain and muscles. As you reflect on your own patterns, you might start to notice whether there are predictable energy crashes and which meals help you feel most steady, focused, and alert.

Blood sugar plays a central role in mood and emotional regulation. When levels are stable, the brain has consistent access to the energy it needs to manage focus, stress, and emotions. When blood sugar drops or rises quickly, such as after skipping meals or eating foods that cause rapid spikes, people may feel irritable, anxious, low, unfocused, or emotionally overwhelmed. Again, these reactions are physiological, not personal shortcomings.

A healthy, well-balanced diet does not look the same for everyone. Cultural preferences, health conditions, access to food, and individual needs all shape what nourishment looks like. While there is no single "perfect" way to eat, a few core principles tend to support both physical and emotional well-being.

Most balanced meals include:

- protein to support muscle repair, satiety, and neurotransmitter production
- carbohydrates, especially complex carbohydrates, for energy and brain function
- healthy fats for hormone production, brain health, and vitamin absorption
- fiber-rich foods to support digestion, blood sugar regulation, and gut health
- a variety of fruits and vegetables to provide essential micronutrients

Rather than aiming for perfection, it's often more helpful to focus on consistency. Small, steady patterns tend to have more impact than doing everything "right" for a short period of time.

A useful question to consider is: *Does this meal support how I want to feel, physically, mentally, and emotionally?* Not perfectly. Just better.

Protein!

Anyone who has ever worked with me knows that I am obsessed with protein.

"Are you eating enough protein?"

"Why don't you try a small amount of protein before you…"

"Would you be willing to try adding a snack with protein?"

Maybe a strange obsession. But once you understand the role protein plays in both physical and mental health, it starts to make a lot more sense.

Understanding the role of nutrition in mental health is not the same as being a nutrition expert. I don't provide individualized dietary recommendations, and I often refer clients to dietitians, nutritionists, or physicians when more specific guidance is needed. If you're unsure what your body needs, consulting a dietitian, nutritionist or physician may also be helpful.

Protein is a fundamental building block of the body. It supports muscle repair, immune function, hormone production, and steady energy. Unlike carbohydrates and fats, the body doesn't store large reserves of protein, which means it needs to be consumed regularly.

It also plays a direct role in mental health. Amino acids, the building blocks of protein, are required to produce key neurotransmitters such as serotonin, dopamine, and norepinephrine. These neurotransmitters are involved in mood regulation, motivation, attention, and stress response. When protein intake is low or inconsistent, the brain may not have the raw materials it needs to support emotional balance. That can show up as low mood, irritability, anxiety, or brain fog.

Consistent protein intake can support more stable energy and mood. This doesn't require perfection or a complete overhaul. Often, small, intentional shifts make a meaningful difference, like including protein at each meal, pairing carbohydrates with protein, or adding a protein-rich snack.

If I had to guess, many of you are probably not getting as much protein as your body actually needs. It takes more intention than most people realize to consistently meet daily protein needs.

General guidelines suggest that adults aim for about 0.8–1.0 grams of protein per kilogram of body weight per day (roughly 0.36–0.45 grams per pound). For example, someone who weighs 150 pounds might aim for approximately 54–68 grams per day to meet basic needs.

Many people fall short simply because protein isn't distributed evenly throughout the day or because meals lean heavily on quick carbohydrates. It can help to think of protein as something to include regularly, not just at dinner. Sources might include eggs, yogurt, beans, lentils, tofu, nuts, seeds, fish, poultry, dairy, or meat—whatever fits your preferences, access, and needs.

Spreading protein intake throughout the day, rather than eating most of it at one meal, can make it easier for your body and brain to use the amino acids they need for energy, mood, and overall functioning.

This does not mean you need to completely overhaul how you eat. Often, small adjustments can make a meaningful difference. Including protein at each meal, pairing carbohydrates with protein to support steadier energy, or adding a protein-rich snack during the day are simple ways to support the brain and body.

Pay attention to how your body responds. Notice the difference between regular meals and skipped meals. Between balanced nourishment and quick fixes. Between steady intake and long gaps without food. The goal here is awareness. Try not to focus on what you *should* be doing, but rather what you are doing currently, and whether it's actually supporting you.

Food is one part of the picture. Hydration is another. And just like nutrition, it's something that affects how you feel throughout the day, often more than you realize.

Hydration

Hydration is another foundational, and often overlooked, part of health. Even mild dehydration can affect energy, concentration, mood, and physical performance. It can also contribute to headaches and that sluggish, foggy feeling that's hard to explain but very noticeable.

About 70% of your brain is made up of water. That's worth paying attention to, because hydration directly supports how your brain communicates, regulates mood, and processes information. When fluid levels drop, even slightly, those systems don't work as efficiently.

Water plays a key role in circulation, digestion, temperature regulation, joint lubrication, and transporting nutrients throughout the body. When hydration is low, the body has to work harder to maintain balance, which can show up as fatigue, brain fog, or just feeling off.

This is one of those areas where people often don't realize what's happening. I've had clients describe feeling tired, unfocused, or more irritable than usual, only to realize later they've had maybe one glass of water all day. Not exactly a fair fight for your brain. You can't sustain life on caffeine, alcohol, and the occasional sip of water.

Even mild dehydration can impact how you feel. It can increase irritability, make stress feel more intense, slow down thinking, and reduce focus. It doesn't create problems out of nowhere, but it can amplify what's already there and make everything feel harder to manage.

Common signs of dehydration include thirst, dry mouth or skin, dark urine, headaches, dizziness, and difficulty concentrating.

Hydration needs vary depending on body size, activity level, climate, medications, and overall health. The goal isn't to follow a rigid rule about how much water you "should" drink. It's to start paying attention and responding to your body.

You might ask yourself:

Do I drink water consistently throughout the day?

Do I sometimes confuse thirst with hunger or fatigue?

How do I feel when I'm actually well hydrated?

Over time, even mild, chronic dehydration can place ongoing stress on the body. It may contribute to fatigue, digestive issues, headaches, muscle cramps, and reduced physical and cognitive performance.

Hydration isn't something to push through or ignore. It's a basic need that supports everything else your body is trying to do.

Sleep is another core system that shapes how you feel, think, and function.

Rest as Regulation

Sleep is not a passive state. It is one of the most active and essential processes your body performs.

While you sleep, your brain organizes information, your nervous system recalibrates, your immune system strengthens, and your hormones reset. Sleep supports emotional regulation, focus, memory, decision-making, and resilience. When sleep is disrupted, nearly every system in the body feels it.

Many people normalize poor sleep, treating it as an inconvenience or something to push through, but sleep is not optional maintenance. It is a biological necessity. It allows the brain and body to regulate emotions, restore energy, consolidate memory, and maintain overall health in ways that simply can't happen while you're awake.

Your body runs on an internal timing system called the circadian rhythm—a roughly twenty-four-hour cycle that regulates sleep and wakefulness, energy, digestion, hormone release, and body temperature.

This rhythm is shaped by light exposure (especially in the morning and evening), consistent sleep and wake times, meal timing, and daily movement. When the circadian rhythm is aligned, sleep tends to feel more natural. You become sleepy at night and feel more alert during the day. When it is disrupted by irregular schedules, late-night screen exposure, shift work, travel, or chronic stress, sleep may become delayed, fragmented, or unrefreshing.

You might notice whether you feel naturally tired at night or wired and alert, whether your sleep schedule is consistent or all over the place, and how much light you're exposed to in the evening

Sleep itself occurs in repeating cycles, each made up of different stages that serve distinct purposes. Light sleep allows the body to begin relaxing, deep sleep supports physical restoration, tissue repair, and immune function, and REM sleep plays a key role in emotional processing, memory consolidation, and creativity.

Over the course of a full night, the body moves through these stages multiple times. Disruptions such as frequent waking, stress, alcohol use, pain, or sleep disorders can reduce the amount of deep and REM sleep you get, even if you spend enough hours in bed. That's why someone can sleep for eight hours and still wake up feeling exhausted.

Notice whether you wake feeling restored or depleted, whether you're waking frequently during the night, or whether mornings feel foggy and slow to start.

Sleep is also deeply connected to hormones and stress. Cortisol, often referred to as the stress hormone, follows a daily rhythm, ideally higher in the morning to help you wake up, and lower at night to allow sleep. Chronic stress can disrupt this pattern, leading to difficulty falling asleep, early morning waking, or that "wired but tired" feeling.

Other hormones play a role as well. Melatonin signals sleep onset and is shaped by light and darkness. Insulin can be affected by late eating and blood sugar fluctuations. Sex hormones shift across the menstrual cycle, pregnancy, postpartum, perimenopause, and menopause. Thyroid hormones influence metabolism and energy.

Sleep challenges aren't always behavioral. Sometimes they're physiological.

You might notice whether you feel physically tired but mentally alert at night, whether stress follows you into bed, or whether sleep changes have lined up with hormonal shifts.

Sleep needs and patterns also change over time. Children and adolescents require more sleep, and teens tend to have later circadian rhythms. Adults often experience lighter sleep and more frequent waking. Life transitions such as parenthood, illness, grief, menopause, and aging, can significantly shift sleep patterns.

It can be helpful to consider how your sleep has changed over time, and whether you're expecting your body to function the way it did in a different phase of life.

Sleep hygiene refers to the habits and environmental conditions that support rest. That might include consistent sleep and wake times, a calming pre-bed routine, less screen exposure at night, a dark and quiet environment, or limiting caffeine and alcohol close to bedtime. Instead of asking what you *should* do perfectly, it's often more useful to ask what makes it easier for your body to rest.

Sometimes sleep issues are a signal that additional support could help. It may be worth speaking with a healthcare provider if you're dealing with chronic insomnia, loud snoring or breathing pauses, persistent daytime sleepiness, restless legs, frequent nightmares, night sweats, or sleep changes connected to mood, pain, or hormonal shifts.

Nearly everyone will experience sleep difficulties at some point.

Struggling with sleep is your body's way of telling you that something may need your attention. It doesn't necessarily mean that anything is wrong. It may reflect increased stress, changes in routine, or an overactive mind. When those stressors are identifiable, there are often practical ways to support your sleep.

Instead of trying to force better sleep, start by noticing what's already happening. When do you feel tired? When do you feel most alert? What is your current bedtime routine? Are there noticeable patterns? The more information you have, the easier it becomes to support your body with sleep in a way that works best for you.

Exercise, or Movement (whichever YOU prefer!)

As a clinician, it's essential for me to use the language that feels right for the person in front of me. That includes how people describe their identity, their experiences, and themselves. It also extends to everyday words we sometimes overlook. I've found there are other terms worth being mindful of in therapy, because my goal is always to be respectful of preferences and use language that feels authentic.

Exercise is one of those words. I've noticed it can elicit a strong reaction.

Many people love this word because it brings up strength, energy and the physical and mental health benefits they associate with it. Others find it triggering because it carries pressure, discomfort, or past experiences that make it harder to engage. I want this section to feel accessible, not alienating, so I'll use *exercise* and *movement* interchangeably.

Exercise offers meaningful benefits for mental health. It can improve mood, reduce stress, and support emotional balance through the release of endorphins and other brain chemicals like serotonin and dopamine. It can also enhance sleep, build confidence, and provide a healthy outlet for managing symptoms of anxiety or depression.

At the same time, many people have learned to view exercise not as care, but as a consequence. Something they "have to do" because of what they ate or how they feel about their bodies. That framing can make movement feel punitive rather than supportive, disconnecting it from its potential to actually improve well-being.

For some people, movement has always been part of life. You may be an amateur or professional athlete, a dancer, a yogi, a pickleball superstar, or someone who values training, discipline, and physical challenge. For others, movement may feel unfamiliar, inconsistent, or disconnected from daily life.

Both experiences belong here.

The question to ask yourself is not *"Do I exercise?"* but *"Is the movement I'm doing supporting me right now?"*

Human bodies are designed for regular movement, though the form and intensity that support health vary widely from person to person. Movement supports circulation and oxygen delivery, joint health and muscle integrity, nervous system regulation, mood and focus, emotional wellbeing, sleep quality, and metabolic health.

For those who move very little, even small amounts of consistent movement can improve energy, mood, and mental clarity. For those who train regularly, balance and recovery are just as essential as effort.

Movement is a physiological need.

Movement also interacts closely with the nervous system, and its effects depend on both the individual and the intensity. For some, movement is calming and grounding. For others, particularly athletes or high performers, it can become activating, obligatory, or even stress-inducing when intensity and recovery are out of balance. Both lack of movement and overtraining can disrupt that balance.

It's worth noticing what movement actually does for you. Does it help regulate stress, or does it add to it? Do you feel restored, energized, or depleted afterward?

When an athlete overtrains, the body and mind often send clear signals that something is off. Physically, they may experience persistent fatigue, decreased performance despite continued effort, muscle soreness that doesn't resolve with rest, increased risk of injury, disrupted sleep, or even changes in appetite and heart rate. What once felt manageable can start to feel unusually difficult or draining.

Emotionally, overtraining can show up as irritability, low mood, increased anxiety, or a sense of burnout. Motivation may drop, and activities they once enjoyed can begin to feel like obligations. Some athletes also report difficulty concentrating or feeling mentally flat. Together, these signs reflect that the body and nervous system are under too much strain and need recovery, not more output.

If movement has long been part of your life, this section of *Empowerful* is inviting you to assess how it currently functions for you. Consider how your training volume aligns with your stress load, whether your recovery is truly adequate, and how sleep, nutrition, and stress interact with your routine.

Reflect on whether movement feels supportive, compulsory, or obligatory. Even disciplined and knowledgeable athletes can drift into patterns of overtraining, under-recovery, or using movement to override exhaustion. Strength includes knowing when to adapt.

For someone who has never exercised before, the idea of starting can bring up a wide range of reactions. You might feel uncertain about where to begin, worry about doing something incorrectly, or feel self-conscious about how you look while moving. Exercise can feel intimidating, especially if it's associated with high intensity or unfamiliar environments like gyms or group classes.

At the same time, you might feel curious or hopeful about the potential benefits, even if those feelings are mixed with hesitation. It's common to feel both interested in change and resistant to it at the same time. When movement hasn't been part of your routine, starting is often less about motivation and more about creating a sense of safety, approachability, and permission to begin in a way that feels manageable.

Different forms of movement support the body in different ways.

Walking and gentle aerobic exercise support circulation, mood, and stress regulation. Strength training supports muscle health and bone density, and has long-term health benefits. Mobility and flexibility work support joint health and injury prevention. Balance and coordination improve stability and confidence. Mind–body practices support awareness and nervous system regulation. Most bodies benefit from variety, but the right mix depends on the individual.

Movement becomes less supportive when it is driven by guilt, fear, compulsion, or rigidity, or when pain, illness, or fatigue are ignored. Signs that movement may be undermining well-being include persistent fatigue, declining performance, sleep disruption, irritability, or recurring injury.

Learning to recognize and listen to these signals is a skill.

As you reflect on your relationship with movement, notice how often you move throughout the day, how your body feels during and after movement, and whether movement feels like care, obligation, or escape. Notice, too, whether stillness feels restorative or uncomfortable. There is no ideal here, only patterns worth understanding.

Stress and the Nervous System

Stress is a normal part of being alive. Your nervous system is constantly scanning both your environment and your internal state, asking a fundamental question: *Am I safe?* The answer to that question shapes nearly everything: your energy, focus, mood, digestion, sleep, immune function, and capacity for connection. When the nervous system senses safety, the body can rest, repair, and adapt. When it senses a threat, even subtly or over long periods of time, the body shifts into protection.

The autonomic nervous system has two primary modes that work together to support survival and balance. The first is activation, often called the sympathetic response, which mobilizes the body by increasing alertness, heart rate, and focus so you can respond to challenges. The second is rest and regulation, known as the parasympathetic response, which supports digestion, immune function, emotional regulation, and restoration. A healthy nervous system moves flexibly between these states. Chronic stress occurs when the system remains activated without enough recovery. Over time, the body can stay in a state of vigilance even when there is no immediate danger.

Chronic stress does not always feel dramatic or obvious. Often, it becomes subtle and normalized over time. It may show up as persistent muscle tension, shallow breathing, irritability or emotional reactivity, fatigue that does not improve with rest, difficulty concentrating, digestive issues, sleep disruption, or feeling exhausted. These are signs of a nervous system that has been carrying a sustained level of demand for too long.

Your body has been trying to get your attention for a while now.

Stress is also not purely psychological. While thoughts and emotions play a role, the nervous system responds to total load rather than mindset alone. Ongoing emotional demands, work pressure, lack of control, relationship strain, financial uncertainty, illness or chronic pain, past or ongoing trauma, sleep deprivation, poor nutrition, and overtraining or under-recovery all contribute. This is why stress management cannot be solved by positive thinking alone.

When the nervous system remains in a state of prolonged activation, capacity often begins to shrink. Energy is diverted away from digestion, immune function, and repair. Emotional regulation becomes more difficult, small problems feel overwhelming, decision-making becomes more reactive, and change can feel exhausting rather than energizing.

Many people interpret this shift as a problem with motivation or discipline, when the real issue is nervous system overload.

Stress responses themselves are adaptive. Fight, flight, freeze, and shutdown developed as ways to keep you safe. The challenge arises when these responses are activated too frequently, too intensely, or for extended periods of time. Understanding your stress patterns creates space for curiosity. You might notice how stress shows up in your body and whether you tend to become reactive, withdrawn, numb, or over-functioning under pressure.

Regulation does not mean being calm all the time. It means being able to mobilize when needed, settle afterward, and return to baseline without force. For some people, slowing down supports regulation. For others, gentle movement, expression, or connection is what helps the system settle.

There is no one-size-fits-all response, only what supports balance for your nervous system.

Supporting the nervous system is less about adding more and more about creating conditions that allow the body to feel safe enough to recover. This might include predictable routines, rhythmic or gentle movement, adequate nourishment and hydration, sufficient sleep, boundaries around overstimulation, connection with safe people, and moments of rest or stillness. Stress is part of life; recovery is what allows the system to sustain it.

Sometimes stress reaches a level where additional support becomes critical. Persistent anxiety or panic, emotional numbness or detachment, ongoing sleep difficulties, chronic pain or unexplained physical symptoms, feeling overwhelmed by everyday tasks, or a sense of being stuck in survival mode are all signals worth paying attention to.

As you reflect on stress and your nervous system, consider what you're noticing rather than what you think should be happening. Pay attention to what activates your system, what helps it settle, and where stress feels manageable versus overwhelming.

Your goal is to understand how the stress you carry affects your nervous system, how your body responds, and how to recognize the difference between healthy activation and chronic overload.

Before You Continue

We've started to *Assess,* by beginning with your physical body. You've been asked to notice how you feel, observe some of your patterns, and explore how your physical health may be impacting your overall well-being with curiosity rather than judgement.

Your body holds context. Past illnesses, chronic conditions, injuries, hormonal shifts, medications, and life experiences all influence how you feel, think, and function. Much of this is invisible to others and easy to dismiss in yourself, yet it still shapes your energy, mood, focus, and capacity every day. Living with ongoing symptoms, even when they are considered manageable, requires energy.

Capacity is shaped by biology just as much as by mindset.

As you reflect on everything we've covered, I encourage you to start seeing your body as a source of information rather than something to push past or fix. Sleep, nourishment, hydration, movement, stress, medical conditions, and medication all influence how much energy and resilience you have available. When these systems are supported, change becomes more accessible. When they are strained, even your best efforts can feel exhausting.

Your body will not be the same in every season of your life. What supported you before may not support you in the same way now.

You are also allowed to be an active participant in your care. You bring the lived experience of your body. Healthcare providers bring training and perspective. When those work together, care becomes more informed, more individualized, and more effective

As you continue through this first part of *Empowerful*, remember that change becomes more sustainable when it is built on reality rather than resistance. Your body is not something you need to override. It is something you can learn to listen to, work with, and support.

That understanding becomes your foundation moving forward.

Pause and Reflect

Take a moment to pause and reflect, without trying to fix or solve anything.

- What signals has my body been sending that I've learned to ignore or push past?
- What would it look like to treat rest, nourishment, and care as requirements rather than rewards?
- Is there something that I consider normal, which may benefit from further exploration?
- Are there any physical needs I've been overlooking that might be affecting my energy, mood, or capacity to change?
- What conditions am I asking myself to change within and are those conditions actually being supported right now?

2

YOUR WORLD

We began by exploring how sleep, nourishment, movement, stress, and physical health influence your energy, mood, and capacity for change. This is only part of the picture. The relationships, roles, environments, and systems you move through each day shape your emotional experience in powerful ways, too.

Sometimes people internalize or personalize difficulties that are actually responses to external conditions. You may think you're unmotivated, anxious, or failing, when in reality you are navigating environments that are stressful, unsupportive, or misaligned with your needs.

Now we widen the lens to assess your world more fully.

Your relationships and environments continuously influence your well-being and your capacity for change. Family, partners, friendships, workplace expectations, cultural messages, community norms, and media all shape how you feel and function. Some of these influences are supportive and empowering. Seeing this clearly helps you place your experiences in context rather than assuming everything begins and ends within you.

Relationships and Environments

You don't live your life in isolation, even if, on some days, you really wish you could.

When I talk to clients about their social network, I'm not asking how many people they know or how busy their calendar looks. I'm interested in connection and influence. Who has access to you. Who you interact with regularly, semi-regularly, or even infrequently, but meaningfully. Who supports you. Who drains you. Who challenges you in ways that help you grow, and who creates tension, stress, or completely exhausts you.

People often assume I'm only asking about close friends or people they enjoy spending time with, but I'm interested in *everyone* who shapes your day-to-day experience: family, partners, coworkers, communities, cultural groups, roles you hold, and environments you move through. Influence doesn't require closeness. Sometimes the most powerful influences are subtle, ongoing, and easy to overlook

This is clinically relevant because relationships affect well-being, plain and simple. Social connections can provide support, safety, and belonging. They can also create stress, pressure, and depletion. They can uplift or undermine. They can empower or constrain. Yes, that's the opposite of empower.

People don't exist in a vacuum, and neither does change. When you change, your world changes with you, sometimes willingly and sometimes not. Think about partners who live together and share routines. If one person receives a health diagnosis that requires dietary changes, that shift doesn't happen in isolation. If cooking together was a shared joy, the other partner is impacted, too. That doesn't make anyone wrong or at fault. It simply reminds us how interconnected we are.

One of the most common relationship patterns I see affecting well-being is perfectionism. It can show up in many ways within relationships. Sometimes it looks like constantly trying to make other people happy at the expense of your own needs or authenticity. Other times it looks like avoidance: avoiding conflict, avoiding uncomfortable conversations, or avoiding situations where someone might feel disappointed. Perfectionism often carries an all-or-nothing quality: worthy or unworthy, good or bad, good enough or terrible. People-pleasing tends to travel right alongside it. When someone feels responsible for maintaining harmony or meeting everyone else's expectations, their own needs can disappear from the equation.

I've also seen many clients discover that their anxiety or stress is strongly connected to a specific relationship dynamic. One example that stands out involved a woman in her fifties and her widowed father. After her mother passed away, she stepped into the role her mother once held: caretaker, emotional support, and primary companion. Her father relied on her heavily, particularly as a place to vent his frustrations and complaints. This client deeply valued what she called "protecting her peace," and the constant negativity left her feeling anxious and depleted. She began dreading his calls, which only increased her guilt and stress. Once she identified the pattern in their relationship, she realized that the only part she could control was her own response. By setting clearer boundaries around what conversations she would participate in, she was able to preserve the relationship while protecting her own well-being.

Even relationships that seem peripheral can have a disproportionate impact on our emotional state. Imagine receiving a message from someone you rarely hear from. How do you react? Are you excited to see their name? Neutral? Or does your stomach tighten because you already anticipate the emotional labor involved in responding?

Our reactions often tell us something meaningful about the patterns in our relationships.

And they invite a useful question: **why do I feel this way?**

Your Environment

Environments shape people over time. Unspoken rules develop. Roles solidify. Communication patterns become familiar. Certain behaviors are rewarded while others are discouraged or punished. Eventually, these patterns start to feel normal.

For example, imagine two different friend groups. One encourages curiosity, disagreement, and respectful conversation across differences. The other leans toward agreement and conformity, where dissent is subtly discouraged. No one may say, "This is how you're supposed to be," but the message still lands.

What feels normal is shaped by the environments we grow up in and the ones we choose, or don't realize we've chosen.

Many unhealthy patterns become normalized simply because they are familiar. A common example I see in clinical practice is the silent treatment. It is often confused with "taking space," but those are very different experiences. Taking space involves communicating a need for time to regulate and then returning to the conversation. The silent treatment involves withdrawing connection as a way of expressing anger, punishment, or control. It is a passive-aggressive form of communication. When someone grows up in an environment where this is common, it may not register as unhealthy until they encounter a different way of communicating.

Some examples are more obvious in hindsight. I've worked with clients who were raised in environments they later described as controlling or "cult-like." Only after exposure to other perspectives did they realize how controlling and narrow those environments had been. Others have shared childhood experiences they once described as funny or normal, only to realize through other people's reactions that they were actually describing neglect, abuse, or trauma.

Another dynamic that often becomes normalized early on is parentification. This happens when a child takes on responsibilities or emotional roles that would normally belong to an adult. That might include caring for younger siblings, managing household responsibilities beyond what is developmentally appropriate, or becoming a primary source of emotional support for a parent.

I once worked with a client who described herself as her single mother's "best friend" growing up. She also helped raise her two younger siblings. For years she believed this arrangement was normal. Only later, with more perspective and support, did she begin to understand the weight she had been carrying as a child.

Those are more extreme examples. Subtle ones show up all the time. Work ethic. Achievement. Money. Emotional expression. What gets praised. What gets ignored. What's expected. What's allowed. Many of us don't realize how deeply these norms shaped us until we step outside them.

I've seen countless clients leave workplaces, family systems, or social environments and suddenly realize how much pressure those environments had been placing on them. Often the stress isn't about the individual. It's about the mismatch between the person and the environment they're in. When that misalignment is constant, it's easy to assume the problem is you rather than the system you've been adapting to.

Another factor worth considering is neurodiversity. Many of the systems that shape modern life are designed with a neurotypical brain in mind. These include schools, workplaces, schedules, and social expectations. Neurodiversity refers to natural variations in how human brains process information, regulate attention, experience sensory input, and interact with the world. People who are autistic, have ADHD, dyslexia, or other neurological differences often move through systems that were not designed with their needs in mind.

When that mismatch exists, individuals may internalize the resulting stress as personal inadequacy. In reality, the strain may be coming from the environment, not the person.

Unwritten Rules

Once you start noticing how environments shape behavior, another layer often becomes visible: the unwritten rules you've been living by.

Every environment carries unspoken rules about how people are expected to behave. We often follow these rules automatically, without realizing they exist. They tend to feel completely normal and reasonable, until you pause long enough to ask what they are costing you.

Take a moment to notice some of the unwritten rules that may be shaping your world. You might write them down in two columns:

Unwritten Rule | Cost

"Work comes before rest." | Burnout, exhaustion

"If I say no, I'm selfish." | Resentment

"We don't talk about conflict." | Avoidance, tension

"I'm the responsible one." | Over-functioning

See what stands out to you, and then begin to consider the cost.

You don't have to change anything yet. Just notice what's been running in the background.

Relationship Circles

Every person exists within layers of relationships.

Some people are at the center of your life. These are the relationships that tend to be emotionally accessible, trusted, and influential. Others exist at a greater distance, where connection may still be meaningful but is shaped more by context, shared roles, or situational contact. Understanding relationships in this layered way can help clarify expectations, support healthy boundaries, and improve overall well-being.

One helpful way to think about relationships is through concentric circles.

Imagine yourself at the center, with rings expanding outward to represent different levels of emotional closeness. The innermost circle includes your closest relationships, those involving trust, vulnerability, and deeper emotional investment. The next layers may include people you care about and feel connected to, but with more selective sharing and clearer boundaries.

Further outward are more role-based or situational relationships, such as coworkers, neighbors, or people you interact with through shared activities or community spaces. These relationships are often shaped more by context than emotional closeness. They can still be positive and supportive, but typically involve less personal disclosure and more defined boundaries.

People can move closer over time. They can also move farther away. This is a natural part of the ebb and flow of relationships.

The goal is to understand where each relationship fits and how it impacts your energy and well-being.

To make this idea more concrete, take a moment to map your current relationships.

Draw a small circle, and place yourself inside that circle. You are at the center. Next, draw a few concentric circles around this one.

- The **inner circle** includes people with the most emotional access to you.
- The **middle circle** includes people who are important but less central to your daily emotional life.
- The **outer circle** includes relationships that are more situational, professional, or occasional.

Write down a few names in each circle. Don't overthink placement. Go with your first honest answer.

Next to each name, add a simple symbol to describe how that relationship affects your energy right now:

+ supportive or energizing

– draining or stressful

± mixed or complicated

You may notice some surprises. A relationship that feels close might also be exhausting. Someone in a more distant circle might actually provide stability or encouragement.

Many people struggle because they give too many people inner-circle access.

There's a saying, expressed in many ways: you can't be everything to everyone, and you shouldn't expect everyone to be everything to you. When we expect the same level of closeness, reliability, or emotional depth from every person in our lives, disappointment becomes almost inevitable.

Understanding relationships for what they are can be incredibly freeing.

I once worked with a client who was devastated that her childhood best friend no longer seemed interested in maintaining the same level of closeness they once had. Their lives had moved in different directions—partners, children, careers, even geography. She felt angry and hurt and believed the friendship had to be either fully restored or ended completely.

Through reflection, she began to see that the relationship still held meaning and history, even if its role had changed. By allowing that friend to move into a slightly more distant circle, she was able to maintain connection without forcing expectations that no longer fit the present reality.

And if I had a dollar for every time someone stayed in a draining relationship out of guilt or obligation, I would be a very wealthy therapist. Slight exaggeration—but you get the point.

Guilt is a powerful moral emotion. Sometimes it comes from external expectations, and sometimes we generate it internally. It can be valid, exaggerated, implied, or entirely imagined. But when guilt becomes the primary reason a relationship continues, it often signals that something deserves a closer look.

Guilt and obligation can be especially complicated within families. Unlike friendships, family relationships are not chosen, and cultural messaging often emphasizes loyalty and permanence. Many people grow up hearing that family must always come first, regardless of how those relationships affect them. These expectations can make it difficult to evaluate relationships honestly, even when they are consistently draining.

With that framework in mind, take a closer look at your current relationships. Consider which might benefit from more intention or care, which boundaries may need clarification, and where additional support could be invited in. At the same time, notice whether some connections deserve reconsideration, not because they are "bad," but because their impact on you may no longer match who you are becoming.

Notice who offers reciprocity and who consistently drains you, who inspires you, and who feels like a black hole of neediness.

Growth shifts dynamics. Some people will respond with interest and encouragement. Others may feel threatened, uncomfortable, or dismissive, sometimes without realizing it. Boundaries allow relationships to remain honest and sustainable, especially when change is underway.

As you continue reflecting, notice who truly belongs in your inner circle and who may fit more appropriately in outer rings. Pay attention to who energizes you and who leaves you depleted, who challenges you in ways that help you grow, and who may unintentionally enable or reinforce patterns you are trying to outgrow.

When you understand the roles people play in your life, you can relate to them with more intention, less resentment, and greater respect for your own capacity.

In my work, I often say: ***"People go to therapy to talk about the people who won't go to therapy."*** That line usually gets a laugh, followed by a knowing nod. Because often, you are the one doing the work. You're the one reflecting, growing, questioning patterns, and wishing that a partner, parent, friend, or colleague would do the same.

And here's the truth: it can be deeply challenging to work on a relationship when the other person isn't in the room. That doesn't mean change is impossible. It does mean that having clarity about the relationship, especially your role in it, is essential.

When You Change, Things Shift

When you begin to change, people notice.

Some will be excited and supportive. Some may feel uncomfortable. Others may resist, not because they want to hurt you, but because your change invites reflection they're not ready for, or disrupts a dynamic that once felt familiar.

One of the most common responses I see when someone begins setting boundaries or changing long-standing patterns is pushback.

Relationships naturally develop a kind of equilibrium over time. People settle into roles, expectations, and familiar ways of interacting. When one person begins behaving differently, by saying no more often, communicating needs more clearly, or no longer participating in old dynamics, it disrupts that balance. In response, people may react with confusion, frustration, or resistance, simply because the system they were used to is changing.

We'll talk more later in *Empowerful* about navigating the friction that can come with growth. But I'll say this gently and clearly here:

Not everybody needs to come with you.

As you grow, align, and change, it becomes appropriate, and sometimes necessary, to reevaluate your relationships. That doesn't mean cutting everyone off. It means being honest about who supports the version of you you're becoming, who may need different boundaries, and who may no longer have the same level of access.

At the same time, I have also seen relationships grow stronger when one person begins doing personal work. Introspection can be powerful. When someone models reflection, accountability, and honesty, it can create space for others to do the same.

Sometimes change creates distance. Sometimes it creates deeper connections.

Emotional Safety and Belonging

Not all relationships offer the same level of emotional safety. Some people allow you to be fully yourself, while others require you to edit, perform, or protect parts of who you are.

Emotional safety means you can be real without fear of punishment, ridicule, withdrawal, or retaliation. It doesn't require constant agreement or ease. Healthy relationships can include disagreement, tension, and difficult conversations. What essential is that everyone in the relationship feels respected, seen, and is able to show up authentically.

Notice where you feel most accepted and understood. Where do you feel judged, minimized, or unseen? And where do you feel lonely, even when you are not physically alone?

Belonging is about being yourself and feeling accepted, not just being around others.

In my experience, people often recognize that a relationship is emotionally unsafe when they begin to question their own perception of reality. They may feel manipulated or gaslit. They may feel chronically guilty, unheard, or drained after interactions. There is often an imbalance in reciprocity within the relationship. Lots of giving, very little receiving. Sometimes these relationships feel transactional, where attention and care are conditional rather than mutual.

Supportive relationships tend to involve reciprocity. Rarely is it a perfect 50/50 split, but there is effort on both sides. Both people give, receive, adjust, and repair. These relationships often feel steady, energizing, and grounding.

Healthy relationships also make space for differences in how people communicate and process emotions. I once worked with a client who needed more time to process difficult conversations with her partner. When a challenging topic came up, she might need hours, or even days, to reflect before responding. Her partner understood this and respected the process. Instead of pressuring her for immediate answers, she allowed space and trusted that the conversation would continue. That flexibility created emotional safety for both of them.

Some relationships are uplifting, enlightening, and expansive. These are the keepers. Others are draining.

And then there are the relationships that *almost* work.

They *almost* meet your needs. They *almost* feel supportive. These can be some of the hardest to evaluate, because hope keeps you invested, even as the relationship wears you down.

On the surface, there may be care, connection, and moments of genuine support. At times you may feel understood or valued, which can make it hard to recognize when something isn't working. These relationships can create confusion because the positive moments make it easy to believe that things will eventually improve, or that the relationship just needs a little more time.

Hope also plays a powerful role in keeping people invested in these dynamics. When there are glimpses of the connection you want, it can feel like proof that the relationship has potential. However, if the overall pattern still leaves you feeling drained, lonely, uncertain, or unsupported, it may be worth paying attention to the pattern over time, not just the best moments.

For example, someone might have a partner who is caring and attentive some days but dismissive or unavailable on others. During the good moments, the relationship feels warm and promising, which makes it easy to overlook the times when emotional needs go unmet. Over time, this cycle can leave a person feeling hopeful yet exhausted, constantly waiting for the relationship to become what it sometimes seems it could be.

Recognizing these types of patterns can be a helpful step towards understanding the relationship for what it actually is, not just what it could be.

Influence Audit: More Than Just People

Your social ecosystem includes more than the people you interact with directly. It also includes the messages, environments, and systems you are exposed to regularly.

Family norms. Inherited beliefs. Cultural expectations. Workplace culture. Media. Social platforms.

These influences shape how you see yourself and the world, often without conscious awareness. They can affect your self-worth, ambition, identity, and sense of what is "normal" or possible. Taking time to examine these influences can help you understand where certain beliefs or expectations came from and whether they still serve you.

Family Norms and Early Influence

Family norms are the spoken and unspoken rules within a family unit. We are often exposed to these patterns early in life, usually as children, and they can start to feel like *"just the way things are."* These norms can shape how emotions are expressed, how conflict is handled, and what roles family members take on.

For example, in some families conflict is addressed openly, while in others it is avoided or suppressed. In some families emotional expression is encouraged, while in others it is minimized or discouraged.

As we grow older and gain experiences outside our family, we sometimes realize that what we assumed was normal may simply be one way of doing things. That realization can create an opportunity to reflect on which family patterns we want to carry forward, and which ones we may want to adjust.

Inherited beliefs often travel alongside these norms. These are the values, expectations, and narratives passed down through families culture, and community. These may come through family stories religious or spiritual traditions, cultural teachings, or everyday messages about how life should be lived.

These beliefs often shape our sense of identity and connection. They can offer meaning, belonging, and continuity. At the same time, some may deserve thoughtful re-examination to determine whether they still align with who you are and the life you want to build.

Cultural and Environmental Expectations

Cultural expectations emerge from the shared norms of a community or group. They shape what is valued, what is rewarded, and how people are expected to behave. They often feel invisible because they are so familiar.

These expectations influence how we define success, how we relate to others, and even how we understand ourselves.

Different cultures emphasize different values. Some place strong importance on family connection, intergenerational responsibility, and community support. Others emphasize independence, personal achievement, or career success. Some prioritize harmony, collective well-being, or connection to the natural world. Many people move between multiple cultural frameworks at once, sometimes seamlessly, and other times with a sense of tension or contradiction depending on the environment they are in.

None of these expectations are inherently right or wrong. But when they go unexamined, they can create pressure that feels personal rather than contextual. You may find yourself striving to meet expectations that don't fully align with who you are, or feeling like you're falling short without fully understanding why.

Taking a step back to notice these influences can help you distinguish between what genuinely feels to you and what has simply been absorbed over time.

I once worked with a client who felt constant pressure to pursue a high-achieving, prestigious career path. On the surface, she appeared successful, but she described feeling disconnected, anxious, and chronically exhausted. As we explored her background, it became clear that many of her choices were shaped by cultural and family expectations around achievement, stability, and status. In her family, there were essentially three acceptable career paths: doctor, engineer, or attorney. Anything outside of those simply wasn't an option.

When she began to reflect on what she actually valued, a very different picture emerged. She was drawn to creativity and expression. She could see herself as a curator, an art historian, or a designer. These were paths that aligned with her interests, but had never felt available. She realized how far her current direction had drifted from what felt authentic. She didn't lack drive or discipline. It was a mismatch between external expectations and internal values.

Workplace Culture

Workplace culture is another powerful influence. It shapes how work gets done, how success is defined, and how people are treated. Some environments encourage collaboration, balance, and respect. Others operate through pressure, competition, or unspoken expectations of constant availability. Sometimes these norms are explicitly stated, but often they are communicated indirectly through behavior, leadership style, and peer influence. Over time, workplace culture can significantly affect stress levels, self-worth, and overall well-being.

Workplace culture is especially impactful because many people spend so much time at work. In many cases, you may see coworkers more frequently than close friends or even family.

And please don't get me started on when company culture insists that their employees are "like one big, happy family."

What makes workplace culture especially tricky is that many of its norms are subtle. They're communicated through behavior, leadership style, and what gets rewarded or overlooked, rather than what is explicitly stated.

Over time, people adapt to these environments, often without realizing it. You may begin to internalize the demands around you, believing you are the problem if you feel overwhelmed, unmotivated, or unable to keep up. In many cases, those reactions have more to do with the environment than with your abilities. They are responses to conditions that may be unclear, unsupportive, or simply mismatched with your needs.

When stress becomes constant, it can start to feel normal. And when that happens, it becomes harder to separate what belongs to you from what belongs to the environment. Taking a step back to assess your workplace with more clarity can help you understand whether the issue is something within you, or something you have been adapting to.

Media

Media influences come from many sources—streaming content, news, advertising, social media, and digital platforms. These messages help shape cultural narratives about what success, beauty, relationships, and happiness should look like.

And it's not just what you choose to consume. It's also what gets served up to you next. Algorithms are constantly filtering and prioritizing content based on what captures your attention, often without you realizing it.

Social media platforms are often described as tools for connection and community. While they can provide meaningful ways to stay in touch with others, they can also create powerful comparison dynamics. Because people tend to share curated highlights of their lives through the sharing of vacations, accomplishments, filtered photos, and happy moments, it can create the illusion that everyone else is doing better, achieving more, or living more fulfilling lives.

At the same time, these platforms are intentionally designed to maximize engagement. Content that triggers strong emotional reactions, such as outrage, fear, conflict, or urgency, tends to spread more quickly than balanced or reflective perspectives. Over time, this environment can shape how you see yourself and the world around you.

This often shows up in subtle but powerful ways. You might notice your mood shift after scrolling, even if you started out feeling fine. You may find yourself comparing your life, your body, your relationships, or your progress to what you're seeing. Even when you logically know the content is curated and selective, your nervous system can still respond as if it's real.

You might also notice how constant exposure to news or high-conflict content leaves you feeling tense, overwhelmed, or on edge. These platforms are designed to capture attention, and emotionally charged content tends to spread quickly. Over time, this shapes not only how you feel, but how you interpret the world around you.

Developing awareness of how media affects your mood, expectations, and self-perception allows you to engage with it more intentionally.

Boundaries, Communication, and Support

Once you begin noticing the influences around you, family norms, cultural expectations, media messages, and relationship dynamics, it naturally raises another question:

Who and what gets access to you?

Growth shifts dynamics. Some people will be curious and encouraging. Others may feel threatened, uncomfortable, or dismissive, sometimes without realizing it. Boundaries allow relationships to remain honest and sustainable, protecting your energy while you continue becoming who you are becoming.

Some people have wide support systems. Some people "collect people" along the way, and I mean that in a very endearing way. Others find deep support through one or two meaningful connections. Support can come in human form, and it can also come from non-human connection. Those of you who love animals know how powerful these bonds can be. (Hello, Bill!)

Growth is often supported by broader connections: mentors, peers, learning communities, and spaces for contribution. These do not replace close relationships. They help to expand your ecosystem.

Consider where you feel encouraged to stretch, where you feel inspired, and where you feel stagnant or disconnected. Being surrounded by people who encourage growth, curiosity, and authenticity can make change feel possible. Environments that reinforce old patterns can pull you back toward what feels familiar.

You are allowed to seek out the people and spaces that support who you are becoming.

Before You Continue

Now that you have started to explore your social ecosystem, you can begin to see how your relationships, roles and environments influence your thoughts, behaviors, and overall well-being. At this stage, it's perfectly okay to simply observe these patterns, with curiosity rather than trying to fix or change anything. Observation itself is a key part of a thorough assessment.

There are many external influences shaping your world. Your family of origin, friends and chosen family, environments, culture, workplace, communities, and the messages you absorb through media are just a few examples. Some of these influences are supportive and encouraging. They uplift you and allow you to show up authentically. Others may feel draining, critical, or simply mismatched with who you truly are.

Perhaps this even gave you a brief opportunity to "blame your parents." (That's a joke.)

More seriously, my hope is that this reflection helps you develop greater self-empathy and compassion as you begin to see how many forces have shaped your early development and who you are today.

As we continue to *assess*, my hope is that the awareness you are building begins to feel empowering. Next, we complete this assessment by exploring your capacity for growth and change.

Pause and Reflect

Take a moment to pause and reflect, without trying to fix or solve anything.

- Which relationships in my life feel supportive, energizing, or grounding?
- Which relationships tend to leave me feeling drained, tense, or overwhelmed?
- Is there a relationship that might benefit from more intention, care, or honesty?
- Where might I be over-giving or under-asking in my relationships?
- Who encourages my growth? Who makes growth harder for me?
- Are there environments that clearly aren't working for me?
- Where and with whom can I be my most authentic self?

3

YOUR CAPACITY

By now, you've spent time looking at two parts of your life: your body and your world. You explored the systems that influence how you feel, and you examined the relationships, environments, and influences that shape your day-to-day experience.

Now, we turn inward in a different way.

This part asks you to understand how you operate, how you show up, why certain patterns repeat, and what capacity you currently have for change and growth. As you move through it, I encourage you to stay curious rather than judgmental. The goal is to understand yourself more clearly and begin to see what may support you best.

Capacity is the amount of emotional, mental, and physical energy you have available to meet the demands of your life. It isn't fixed. It shifts depending on what is happening in your world. Stress, sleep, health, responsibilities, life events, and the emotional or cognitive load you're carrying all affect how much capacity you have available at any given time.

As you assess your capacity, I want you to look at it through four lenses: your strengths, your fit, your load, and your limits.

Before you push yourself to change, it helps to ask:

What am I good at?

What drains me?

What am I carrying?

What does reality allow right now?

That's exactly what we're going to do next.

Capacity

Capacity refers to what you are realistically able to handle at a given moment, based on everything currently happening in your life. It includes your time, energy, emotional bandwidth, responsibilities, stress level, and available support.

When someone wants to make a change, it helps to take an honest look at all of these factors, not just the desire to change. You might want to add something new, improve a habit, or take on a goal, but the more useful question is this: does it actually fit into your life right now, or does it create friction.

If your schedule is already full, your energy is low, and your stress is high, adding more may not be about discipline. It may be a mismatch in capacity. Understanding that helps you make adjustments that are realistic and sustainable, rather than pushing yourself into patterns that lead to overwhelm, burnout, or giving up altogether.

Everyone has a certain level of capacity at any given time. When the demands of life exceed it, people often begin to feel overwhelmed, exhausted, irritable, or shut down. Sometimes capacity can be restored through rest, support, meaningful connection, or stepping away from constant demands. But there are usually many systems working together to determine how much energy is actually available to you.

Many people assume that when they are struggling to keep up, the answer is simply to try harder.

One moment I see often in my clinical work is when someone realizes that the problem isn't laziness or lack of motivation. The problem is that they have been expecting themselves to operate at a level that is simply unsustainable, as if they had more time, energy, or support than they actually do. I often give a treadmill example: you can likely walk at level three for longer than you can sprint at level ten, right? And then see what happens when you add an incline!

I have worked with many high-achieving people over the years including college and professional athletes, executives, other highly successful professionals, and people who have built their identity around pushing themselves to perform. Many of them have been taught that when something isn't working, the solution is to push harder, work longer, or "put their game face on."

But grit is not always the solution.

Sometimes the real issue is that the system someone is operating within does not match what a human can sustainably carry. There may be a gap between what someone can realistically bring and what the environment expects of them.

One of my favorite moments in therapy is what could be called the **"It's not me, it's ________" moment.**

This is when a client begins filling in the blank with the reality of their situation.

It's not me, it's my job.

It's not me, it's my family dynamic.

It's not me, it's the system I'm operating in.

It's not me, it's unrealistic expectations.

Occasionally someone will land on: *"It's not me, it's end-stage capitalism."*

(That one tends to get a rueful laugh from me.)

More seriously, moments like this often bring a sense of relief. When people realize the issue isn't personal, that it may be systemic, situational, or influenced by something outside of them, self-blame and shame tend to ease. In their place, something more useful emerges: clarity about what is actually within their control. That shift can feel empowering.

It's a very different experience than assuming everything is your fault.

Because the truth is, you did not arrive at this moment randomly. Your skills, coping strategies, habits, fears, and strengths developed in response to real experiences—family systems, cultural expectations, opportunities and losses, responsibilities, and long-standing demands.

When you understand how and why you operate the way you do, something shifts. You stop trying to change yourself through force and begin designing change that actually fits your real life.

As you continue to *assess*, I'll again encourage you to write things down rather than simply thinking about them. Capturing your observations makes them easier to revisit and build on, and many of the insights you gather here will become useful as you begin aligning your values and activating meaningful change.

Strengths

Strengths are the internal resources, personal qualities, and abilities you already have within you. They influence how you respond to challenges, relate to others, and show up in your day-to-day life. These might include things like resilience, creativity, kindness, problem-solving, or the ability to ask for support. They're the parts of you that are already working, even if you don't always notice or give yourself credit for them.

By definition, strengths include the qualities that support how you cope, adapt, and grow. They can be skills, traits, tendencies, or internal resources that come more naturally, feel more sustainable, or have helped you navigate challenges over time. Strengths are not the absence of weaknesses, and they're not limited to achievement or performance.

They show up in many forms:

- Emotional capacities, like empathy, patience, or resilience.
- Cognitive styles, like problem-solving, creativity, or perspective-taking.
- Behavioral patterns, like persistence, reliability, or flexibility.
- Relational abilities, like attunement, humor, or boundary awareness.

One thing to understand is that strengths are often context-dependent, not absolute. A quality that serves you well in one situation may become less helpful in another. For instance, being independent and self-reliant can foster confidence, yet under strain it may turn into isolation or a reluctance to ask for help. In a similar way, being optimistic and positive can boost resilience, but in more difficult moments it might lead to minimizing problems or avoiding hard emotions.

Seeing strengths this way moves us away from labeling people as "strong" or "weak" and toward understanding how different qualities operate, adapt, and can be used intentionally. You already have tools in your toolbox. The question becomes which ones you reach for, and when.

This is the first lens to look through as you're exploring your capacity.

When you understand what is already working, you stop trying to build something completely from scratch and start building from a foundation which already exists.

Sustainable growth comes from understanding who you already are and how you became this way. It comes from knowing your strengths, limitations, habits, and the path that brought you here. You are not a blank slate. You are not starting over. You are working with a real person who has lived a real life.

Your lived experience has shaped how you respond to stress, pursue goals, manage relationships, and attempt change. Family systems, culture, opportunities and losses, responsibility, trauma, support, and constraint have all played a role. None of this happened randomly. Many of the patterns you struggle with today once helped you survive, adapt, or belong.

If you're someone who thinks visually or creatively, you may appreciate this metaphor: you are not a blank canvas. You are beginning to create your masterpiece on something that already has marks on it. There are layers, textures, maybe even parts you wish weren't there, but this is the canvas you're working with. You don't get to start from scratch, so the work becomes learning how to rework what already exists.

Two people can want the same outcome, attempt the same process, and have completely different experiences with it… not because one is more motivated or capable, but because their capacity, context, and patterns are different. So are their strengths.

When you understand your own system, you stop treating yourself like a problem to solve and start working with what's *already working well.* For many people, this understanding brings relief. It replaces self-blame with context and turns *"What's wrong with me?"* into *"Of course this makes sense."*

Now, it's time to talk about YOUR strengths.

For some of you, this will feel comfortable, natural, maybe even a little satisfying. For others, this part may feel awkward, uncomfortable, or oddly hard. And if that's you, it probably means this section is for you.!

So let me ask you something…

If I asked you to name your top ten strengths, your superpowers, what would you say?

These are the qualities that help you function, cope, adapt, survive, or thrive. The things you've developed over time or intentionally cultivated. The parts of you that *work*.

What is good about you? What genuinely works well for you? And no, you are not allowed to say "nothing", because that's simply not true. It may *feel* true at this moment, but remember: feelings aren't facts.

So if you're stuck, borrow perspective. What would a friend say about you? A colleague? Someone who relies on you? Or your cat. (Animals tend to have very clear opinions. Looking at you, cats!)

Please don't move on from this section until you can name **at least one** strength. Perhaps take some time to journal or write down a few, or as many as you can think of.

Yes, I know I'm being a little pushy here, but I really believe there's value in identifying something good about you. Some of you will write a robust list without breaking a sweat. Others will stare at the page like it personally offended you. Don't be concerned with whichever one you are because both experiences are normal.

And just to be clear: the person who struggles to name one strength does not have fewer strengths than the person who can list ten.

Fit vs. Friction

Fit is the second lens through which to explore capacity.

Fit refers to how well your environment, expectations, and demands align with how you naturally function. When there is a good fit, things tend to feel manageable. Not necessarily easy, but doable. You may still be challenged, but the effort feels productive rather than draining. You're able to follow through more consistently, recover more easily, and show up as yourself without having to force it.

. . .

Friction is what you feel when there is a mismatch. It shows up as unnecessary effort, frustration, or a sense that something is harder than it should be. You're pushing against your natural tendencies, overriding your needs, or forcing yourself into a way of operating that doesn't quite work for you.

Friction can also occur when what you're trying to do doesn't match the reality of the situation.

Sometimes this has less to do with who you are and more to do with the system you're operating within. For example, you might want to become more efficient at work, improving your routine and how tasks are completed. But your job is inflexible and requires you to be there for eight hours. Period. You can become as efficient as possible, but the friction remains because the structure itself doesn't change.

Or imagine trying to improve your morning routine. You decide you want slower, more intentional mornings. But lunches still need to be made, kids still need help getting out the door, and the bus still comes at the same time. Again, friction. Not because you're doing something wrong, but because you're trying to change something without fully accounting for the reality around it.

Fit requires working with reality, not against it.

Having an understanding of who you are and how you operate can make all the difference when you're designing change. That way you're creating something that will work for YOU. Not for your friend, your coworker, or the person you saw online.

Your personality, temperament, and working style shape how you process information, make decisions, handle risk, respond to structure or flexibility, manage stimulation and downtime, and experience energy throughout the day.

Some people thrive on routine, while others need variety. Some think out loud, while others need time to process internally. Some are energized by collaboration, others by solitude. There are many different ways of functioning. The issue arises when there is a mismatch between who you are and what is being asked of you.

When those mismatches persist, they're often personalized as something wrong with you, when in reality, they're signs of misalignment.

I once worked with a client who was deeply introverted by nature but held a job that required her to be "on" all day; constant interaction, constant responsiveness, constant engagement. By the end of each workday, she felt completely depleted. There was nothing left to give. This exhaustion began to spill into her relationship, where her partner felt neglected and confused by her withdrawal. Changing jobs wasn't an option. But changing *expectations* was.

Once there was a shared understanding that she needed a brief period of decompression after work, everything shifted. Fifteen minutes of silence with no conversation and no demands, was enough to restore her capacity. She wasn't avoiding her partner. She was regulating her nervous system. The relationship improved because her needs were acknowledged and honored.

Another client noticed that she shut down during difficult conversations with her partner. Under pressure to respond quickly, she would retreat or agree just to end the discomfort. What looked like avoidance was actually a slower processing speed. Once she understood this, she was able to name it: she needed time to think before responding. When she communicated this directly, her partner felt relieved and appreciated the honesty far more than premature agreement or emotional withdrawal.

These examples highlight something important: what we often label as a problem or personal flaw may actually be a signal.

If you are experiencing friction in the form of stress, strain, unnecessary pressure, or constant struggle, it may be worth exploring whether something about the situation simply isn't working well for you. Understanding what creates friction can help you figure out what fits better.

This is the real value of paying attention to fit and friction. It gives you useful information and helps you ask better questions: What feels off here? What is creating so much effort? What, if it changed, would make this situation feel more manageable, sustainable, or natural?

Sometimes the issue is simply a mismatch between how you function and what is being asked of you.

In each of these examples, what looked like a personal flaw was actually a clue that something else was going on. What looked like avoidance, withdrawal, or difficulty was useful information. Once that information was understood, the person could respond differently and make changes that fit them better.

Ways of understanding how you're wired can be helpful when they give you language to better understand yourself. Think of them as tools for awareness, not definitions of who you are. The goal is to use that insight to make choices, set expectations, and build routines and relationships that work with you rather than against you.

Write this down before moving on:

Where does my life currently feel like a poor fit?

Where am I spending energy compensating instead of aligning?

What feels draining, not because it's hard, but because it's mismatched?

The Invisible Load

The third lens to view capacity through is your load: everything you are carrying, both visible and invisible, that requires your time, energy, and emotional bandwidth. This includes responsibilities you can easily point to, like work or caregiving, as well as the ones that often go unnoticed: planning, anticipating, managing emotions, and holding things together behind the scenes.

When your mental, emotional, and cognitive load is high, your capacity naturally decreases. Everything you're carrying requires time, energy, and attention. As much as I hate to break it to some of you, those resources are limited. That can mean there isn't space to take on anything more, or that the space you do have is much smaller than you'd like.

With that in mind, it also helps to consider where the overall workload is coming from.

Work is a powerful influence on how we feel, function, and define ourselves and not all work is paid. Caregiving. Parenting. Household management. Emotional labor. Community responsibility. Advocacy. Cultural or religious obligations. Much of this labor is invisible, undervalued, and deeply taxing. It requires constant attention, problem-solving, emotional regulation, and follow-through.

Unpaid labor refers to the work people do without financial compensation that is nonetheless essential to families, communities, and society. This includes caring for children, partners, aging parents, or family members with chronic health needs; managing households; volunteering; organizing; and meeting cultural or religious expectations. While this work can be meaningful and deeply aligned with values, it still consumes time, energy, and emotional capacity.

When this labor goes unnamed or unacknowledged, people often blame themselves for feeling exhausted, resentful, or depleted, when the reality is that they are simply carrying more than most people see.

I've worked with clients whose lives were shaped almost entirely around invisible labor.

There are many forms of invisible labor that people don't count as real work. I see this often with caregivers—parents of young children, adult children caring for aging parents, and partners of people living with disabilities or chronic health conditions. Much of this work happens in the background. It includes anticipating needs, managing logistics, monitoring emotional states, adjusting plans, remembering details, and carrying ongoing responsibility for other people's well-being.

Because this labor is rarely measured or formally acknowledged, it's easy to underestimate how much capacity it consumes. People often tell themselves they "should" be able to do more, without fully recognizing how much they are already managing.

One client was the primary source of income for her household while also supporting a partner with chronic health issues. During flare-ups, both physical and emotional, she provided constant care. She made meals, cleaned the house, ran errands, managed appointments, and was responsible for what I jokingly refer to in my own home as *the trifecta*: dishes, laundry, and trash.

On top of that, she carried the mental load: tracking what needed to be done, anticipating needs, and holding everything together. She came to therapy wondering why she was so exhausted and irritable, convinced she was "just not coping well." In reality, she was working multiple full-time jobs, most of which had no official title, no paycheck, and no time off.

Another client, an older adult, had spent years caring for a partner with a chronic illness. Over time, caregiving became his primary identity. When we began talking about his own needs, he said quietly, "I don't know who I am anymore." He had simply done so much caring for her, without respite, that there was little room left for anything else.

Even work that is chosen and meaningful can become draining when boundaries are unclear. Volunteer work, advocacy, and community involvement can provide purpose, connection, and fulfillment. At the same time, they require time, energy, emotional investment, and limits, especially when the work involves care or exposure to others' suffering.

Meaning and purpose do not eliminate the need for rest.

I hope that you will acknowledge the *full scope* of what you carry, the paid and unpaid, visible and invisible. You don't need to minimize it or explain it away. Much of this labor is unseen, undervalued, and often unpaid.

When labor goes unnamed, capacity gets misjudged. And when capacity gets misjudged, people often blame themselves for not doing more.

The Limits of Reality

The fourth lens to view your capacity through is your limits. These are the realities you are living with that shape what is possible for you right now. In my clinical work, I often talk with clients about these limits, and I refer to them as the *limitations of reality*. These are the concrete, non-negotiable factors that shape your life and your options.

These limitations include things like time, money, health, energy, family responsibilities, education, employment, access to resources, and caregiving demands.

The reason I call them the *limitations of reality* is because these are the conditions you must work within, rather than against, to achieve the best possible outcome. If you ignore them or try to work around them, the solution probably won't work very well. Whether you acknowledge them or not, they are already influencing your choices, your outcomes, and the amount of effort required to make any change.

Ignoring these constraints does not create growth. It creates burnout.

These realities need to be named clearly because any attempt to grow, improve, or problem-solve has to be built from the ground you are actually standing on. When these realities aren't accounted for, plans may look good on paper but fall apart in practice. The issue usually isn't motivation or capability. The plan simply wasn't aligned with real life.

Working within these limits does not mean giving up on change. It means making change possible.

This is where I see many clients turn their frustration inward. When something doesn't hold, it's easy to assume the issue is personal, without considering whether the system itself is part of the constraint.

I've worked with clients whose struggles were clearly shaped by structural barriers rather than personal shortcomings. One example that stands out is a highly driven school administrator who was deeply self-critical because she could not achieve the outcomes she wanted for her school. As we looked more closely, the barriers became clear: she needed more experienced teachers, an assistant who worked with her rather than against her, and a supervisor who understood the realities of serving an underserved school community rather than comparing it to high-achieving schools with very different resources.

Once she recognized that she could work day and night, give a thousand percent effort, and still be limited by the conditions around her, something shifted. She didn't like those limitations, and she still wanted change, but directing that frustration at herself no longer made sense.

Designing change without accounting for limits often leads people to feel inadequate, even when they are doing their absolute best. When effort doesn't produce results, the assumption is often that *I must not be trying hard enough*, rather than *this plan doesn't fit my reality*.

It's also essential to acknowledge that reality is not neutral or evenly distributed.

Many of the challenges people face are shaped not only by personal choices but by broader social systems often referred to as "isms." These include racism, sexism, ageism, ableism, socioeconomic classism, heteronormativity, discrimination related to gender identity or expression, religious discrimination, and other forms of systemic inequity. These systems influence who has access to safety, opportunity, healthcare, education, financial stability, and social support and who is forced to work harder just to maintain footing.

Often, the effects of these systems are subtle and cumulative. They show up as chronic stress, increased vigilance, barriers to care, constrained choices, and internalized messages about worth or capability. Over time, they shape health, self-perception, energy, and sense of belonging.

Naming these influences helps provide context.

When social realities are acknowledged, personal struggles can be understood more accurately, not as personal failure, but as adaptive responses to unequal conditions. This perspective allows for compassion, realism, and more sustainable planning.

When clients finally recognize a contextual limit instead of treating it as failure, something often shifts emotionally. Self-criticism softens. The judgment eases. There is often relief in realizing that the issue is not simply personal, but also shaped by the system they are operating within.

Rather than fighting against reality, people can begin moving toward acceptance, which is something I define carefully with clients. Acceptance does not mean liking something, choosing it, approving of it, or wanting it to happen again. It simply means you are no longer spending your energy fighting the fact that it exists. That shift reduces friction and opens the door to more honest, solution-focused strategies.

Working with reality, rather than fighting it, is how change becomes possible. When you understand your limits clearly, you stop designing change based on who you wish you could be and start designing it based on what your life can actually support, *right now*.

Before You Continue

By now, you've taken a deeper look at your capacity through your strengths, fit, load and limits.

Your strengths are what supports you.

Your fit is how your environment matches you.

Your load is the mental, emotional and cognitive tasks that you carry.

Your limits are what reality will allow at this time.

Recognizing how these factors interact can give you a clearer picture of what you can realistically take on.

Along the way you may have noticed something: many of the things people criticize themselves for begin to make so much more sense when they are viewed in context. The habits, strategies, and behaviors you have did not appear randomly. They developed in response to real experiences: family systems, cultural expectations, responsibilities, opportunities, losses, and the environments you move within.

For some people, simply identifying what needs to change is enough. For others, understanding *why* they operate the way they do is an essential part of the process. When you begin to see both the **how** and the **why** behind your patterns, something shifts. Self-criticism softens. Curiosity grows. What once felt like personal failure often reveals itself as adaptation.

And when you understand your strengths, limits, patterns, history, and constraints, the question naturally begins to change. Instead of asking, *"Why can't I just try harder?"* you begin asking a much more useful question:

"What would actually work for me?"

That shift is powerful. Sustainable change happens when you work within the limits of your reality and design change that fits who you are, what you carry, and the conditions you are living within.

Over the last three chapters, you've examined the core pieces of your current reality: your body, your world, and your capacity. Together, these form the foundation of a thorough assessment.

As we arrive at the end of the first part of *Empowerful*, you now have a clearer picture of the landscape you're standing in. You've taken the time to understand the systems influencing your well-being, the relationships and environments shaping your experiences, and the capacity you have available right now.

Now that the assessment is complete, we begin to *align*, examining the values, thoughts, and beliefs that will help to guide the changes you want to make.

Pause and Reflect

Take a moment to pause and reflect, without trying to fix or solve anything.

- What are the *limitations of reality* shaping your life right now?
- Which constraints have you been treating as personal failures instead of contextual limits?
- Where might your expectations of yourself be misaligned with your current capacity?
- What feels genuinely non-negotiable — and what might be open to adjustment?
- Are there social, cultural, or systemic factors that help explain why certain things feel harder than they "should"?
- Which expectations, yours or others', may need to be adjusted?

PART II

ALIGN

Your Values • Your Narrative • Your Thoughts

In the first part of *Empowerful*, you examined where you are - your body, your world and your capacity. Once you understand where you are, the next step is to *align* where you're going.

Alignment connects your values, goals, and daily choices so your life no longer feels like it's pulling in competing directions. When alignment is present, clarity increases and friction decreases. Instead of forcing change or pushing against yourself, what you're doing begins to reflect what's most important to you.

We begin by identifying your core values. These are the principles and priorities that guide how you want to live. You'll explore what is of the utmost importance to you, not based on expectations, roles, or external pressure, but on what feels meaningful and authentic. These values become a reference point, helping you evaluate decisions, behaviors, and commitments as you move forward.

From there, we'll explore the narratives you hold about yourself and the world around you. These stories shape how you interpret experiences, relate to others, and imagine what's possible. Some of them may still serve you well. Others may be outdated or limiting. Together, we'll look at which stories still fit and which may need revision.

As these narratives come into focus, you may uncover deeply held beliefs about yourself. Some will be supportive and grounding. Others may no longer reflect who you are or who you're becoming. Letting go of unhelpful beliefs isn't about judgment or self-criticism; it's about understanding where they came from and deciding, with self-empathy and honesty, whether they still belong.

Finally, we'll look at patterns of thinking that may be contributing to distress. Cognitive distortions are common ways of interpreting the world that can shape emotions, behaviors and sense of possibility. These patterns are learned, and because they are learned, they can also be changed. With awareness and practice, you can begin to notice them and respond differently.

The goal of this section is to bring your values, beliefs, and thoughts into alignment so they reflect who you are and how you want to live.

4

YOUR VALUES

Core values are the guiding principles that shape your decisions, influence your behavior, and define how you move through your life. They are different from goals, preferences, or the external messages you've received along the way.

You can think of your values as a compass. They provide direction when you're faced with decisions, challenges, or uncertainty. In my work, I often return to values as a reference point, something to help people decide how they want to respond in a situation, how they want to show up in relationships, and what truly matters when choices feel complicated.

At a broader level, values connect to something bigger:

How do you want to be known?

How do you want to be remembered?

How do you want to show up in your life?

When there is alignment between what you value and how you live, things tend to feel clearer and more grounded. When there is misalignment, it often creates friction, which can show up as resentment, stress, exhaustion, or even burnout. That tension is often a signal that something meaningful is being overlooked or overridden.

Values also anchor your boundaries and decisions. They help you determine what to say yes to, what to say no to, where to spend your time and energy, and how to navigate difficult or imperfect situations.

The challenge is that many people are not living from values they've consciously chosen. Instead, they're operating from values that were inherited, absorbed, or shaped by external messages—what they were taught they *should* value, rather than what actually feels true to them. Over time, this can create a sense of disconnection from your authentic self, or the feeling that you're playing a role rather than living your life.

As you begin to *align*, you'll start by clarifying your own values. You'll define what's important to you, what gives your life meaning, and what you want your choices to reflect. You'll learn how to use your values as a framework for decision-making, boundaries, and alignment in your daily life.

Once your values are clear, they don't just guide you. They also support you. They become the structure that helps you decide how to spend your time, who you spend it with, what you choose to do (and not do), and how you show up, especially in the moments that matter most.

Core Values

Your values shape your life, whether you're aware of them or not. They influence the decisions you make, the boundaries you set (or avoid), your behaviors, and the stories you tell yourself about what is possible.

Core values are the deeply held beliefs and qualities that guide how a person wants to live their life. They represent what is most meaningful to someone at their core and can serve as an internal compass when making decisions, facing challenges, or choosing between different paths. Values might include things like honesty, family, growth, compassion, creativity, or independence. Unlike external pressures or expectations from others, core values come from within and reflect the kind of person someone wants to be and the way they want to show up in the world.

When individuals understand their values, they often gain clarity about why certain situations feel meaningful or uncomfortable. Values do not provide one single "correct" answer, but they can help guide actions in ways that feel authentic and purposeful. Even during difficult moments, returning to core values can help people move forward in ways that feel aligned with the life they want to build.

When life feels confusing, draining, or misaligned, it's possible that what you're doing isn't connected to what actually aligns with you.

When I talk about core values with clients, I'm talking about the things they care deeply about: how they want to show up in the world, what they want to stand for, what they prioritize when things get hard, and what they look for in themselves and in others.

Values reflect who you are, not who you think you're supposed to be.

Goals, Preferences and Expectations

People often confuse values with goals, preferences, or expectations, so it helps to understand the difference.

Goals are specific outcomes or achievements you might work toward. They often involve clear steps or milestones, such as completing a task, starting a project, improving a relationship, or developing a healthier routine. While values represent ongoing directions for living, goals are more concrete and can be completed or accomplished. In many ways, goals are how values become visible in action. For example, someone who values growth might set a goal to learn a new skill or pursue additional education

Preferences are the things that you like, enjoy, or choose when given options. They can include your tastes, interests, or ways of doing things that feel comfortable or appealing. For example, someone might prefer working independently rather than in large groups, or they might prefer quiet environments over busy ones. Preferences are often flexible and may change over time or depending on the situation. While they can influence decisions, preferences are usually more flexible than core values and they may change over time or shift depending on circumstances.

Expectations are the beliefs or assumptions that people have about how situations, relationships, or outcomes should unfold. These expectations may come from personal experiences, cultural influences, or messages learned from family and society. Sometimes expectations can be helpful by providing structure or motivation. However, when expectations become rigid or unrealistic, they can lead to disappointment, frustration, or pressure. Exploring expectations can help people develop more balanced and flexible perspectives, allowing them to respond to situations with greater understanding and self-compassion.

Values run deeper than all of these. They are ongoing, lived principles - things such as connection, honesty, growth, creativity, stability, compassion, and integrity. You don't "complete" a value. You live it, over and over, through daily choices.

Borrowed Values and the Problem with "Should"

And yet, when people hear the word *values*, many immediately think of what they *should* value.

There are a lot of voices in the world telling us how we should live, what we should want, what success should look like, how we should act, love, work, parent, or relax. We're going to discuss the problem with "should" in depth later in the *Align* section, but for now, let's just acknowledge that it is a powerful word which can create all sorts of issues when people listen to its messages. It's easy to absorb those messages without ever consciously choosing them.

Borrowed values often look good on the surface, but they tend to create burnout, resentment, or a constant sense of friction. You might be doing all the "right" things and still feel disconnected, exhausted, or oddly dissatisfied. That tension is often a sign that your values and your behavior are out of sync.

Sometimes values need to be redefined.

Imagine believing you must value "family," while growing up in a family where you experienced emotional neglect or abuse. That creates enormous internal conflict. But when you're allowed to redefine that value, from *family of origin* to *chosen family*, things begin to make sense. Loving and committing to the people you intentionally choose feels very different than forcing loyalty to people who continue to harm you.

Clarity

Things tend to shift when someone becomes clear about their core values.

Thinking sharpens. Decisions feel more grounded. Life starts to feel more authentic and intentional. Actions begin to align with who you are.

Clarity is powerful. It can reconnect someone who has been going through the motions with who they really are. Anyone who has ever lived behind a mask, or tried to be a version of themselves that didn't quite fit, knows how exhausting that can be.

Values also become clear through misalignment.

Imagine being in a relationship with someone who prefers to stay indoors while you feel most alive outside. Neither person is wrong. But if you find yourself chronically unhappy, trying to change your partner, or shrinking your own needs, there may be an issue with core values.

Or consider a career that demands sixty-plus hours a week in a competitive environment focused on advancement, when you're someone who works to live rather than lives to work. Many people thrive in that setting. But if you don't, this is a significant misalignment.

When people aren't living in alignment with their values, conflict shows up, both internally and externally. Stress, irritability, guilt, resentment, anxiety, and a sense of being pulled in too many directions are common signals.

Alignment doesn't mean life becomes easy, but it often brings steadiness and integrity. You may still face challenges, but you're no longer working against your own internal compass.

Discovering Your Values

One exercise I often use with clients is working backward from the end of life, not in a morbid way, but in a clarifying one.

How would you want to be remembered by family, friends, and colleagues?

What qualities would you want people to name?

If there are accomplishments you hope to be remembered for, what personal qualities made those possible?

Values are often embedded in the answers to these questions.

They can also reveal themselves through patterns. Peak moments, such as times when you feel proud, fulfilled, or most like yourself, often point directly to what you value. Conversely, so do moments of deep resentment. Both perspectives are informative.

When a client tells me, "I don't know what my values are," we need to start somewhere. Sometimes that means reviewing a list and noticing what stands out. Sometimes it means looking at what they're exhausted by just as much as what they're drawn toward.

I might ask them to choose a few values that resonate and then reflect on a time they lived one of those values, what it felt like, what the impact was, and what changed because of it.

Occasionally, values work comes with resistance or discomfort. It can be unsettling to realize how long you've lived out of alignment. People may feel grief, anger, confusion, or fear about what change might require. Sometimes staying uncomfortable feels safer than making the changes needed to realign, especially when realignment involves boundaries, disappointment, or letting others down.

And this is where values work moves from reflection into something more concrete.

I once worked with a client who was struggling with perfectionism and an impossibly packed schedule. When she told me her goal was to "relax on the couch and read a book," we both laughed. That wasn't her. Relaxing on the couch was a metaphor for choosing herself, not a literal activity that she would enjoy. She wasn't a "curl up quietly" person. She was a roller derby and rappel from a cliff kind of person.

Once we clarified that she valued excitement, achievement, and momentum, rather than stillness for its own sake, the work became much more honest and doable. Choosing herself didn't mean slowing down. It meant intentionally making room for the things that actually felt like *her*.

Your version of "choosing yourself" may look very different. You might take a moment to explore what that actually looks like *for you*.

Another client demonstrated what values look like in action through a specific interaction. He had already identified that he wanted to be firm but kind in his relationships. At the time, he was feeling irritated with his brother-in-law, who repeatedly used a childhood nickname he had asked him not to use.

He wanted to think through how to respond the next time it happened. Rather than reacting out of frustration, he chose to respond in alignment with his values. When the moment came, he said, "I'm glad we're family, but that nickname is reserved for two people, and brother, you aren't one of them!", delivering it with a reassuring smile. He was clear, direct and kind.

Alignment often looks like this: small, intentional choices made consistently.

Core values serve as anchors. And if we're leaning into a nautical metaphor, they're also lighthouses—steady points of reference that guide you through rough waters. They don't remove storms, but they help you navigate them without drifting off course.

The rest of the work in *Empowerful* will ask you to return to your values again and again. They become a reference point for decisions, boundaries, and change.

Values point you toward the kind of life you want to live. So before you move on, I encourage you to spend some time thinking about what matters the most to you.

Before You Continue

Your core values shape how you live and who you become. Living in alignment doesn't mean life becomes easy or conflict-free. It means your decisions begin to feel clearer and more intentional. Your actions reflect the kind of person you are or who you want to be.

There is a cost to living out of alignment. When your behaviors, choices and responses don't reflect your values, friction increases. That friction shows up as resentment, exhaustion, frustration or a feeling that *something isn't right.*

Identifying your values gives you an incredibly useful tool: a decision-making roadmap. A guide you can return to when you are faced with a choice, decision or find yourself in need of direction. This is especially useful when life feels uncertain. Knowing your core values can help guide how you respond, how you set boundaries, and how you choose between competing demands.

Of course, this isn't always straightforward. The world is full of messages about what we *should* value, how we *should* behave, and what our lives *should* be like. These *"shoulds"* can pull us away from our authentic selves and create misalignment.

My hope is that through this process you've become not only curious about your values, but excited about them and what they might mean for your life and for your legacy.

These are yours to define.

And yet, even when people know their core values and who they want to be, sometimes there is a struggle, an internal conflict, because deeply held stories continue to shape them. Stories that may or may not be true. Stories that may need a revision.

That's where we're going next.

Pause and Reflect

Take a moment to pause and reflect, without trying to fix or solve anything yet.

- Which values feel most alive for me right now, even if I'm not fully living them yet?
- Where in my life do I feel most aligned? What am I doing, or not doing, when I feel that way?
- Where do I feel tension, resentment, or exhaustion? What value might be getting ignored or overridden there?
- Which values might I be living because they were expected of me, rather than chosen by me?
- When have I felt most like myself in the past year? What values were present in those moments?
- If I made decisions from my values instead of my "shoulds," what might shift—even slightly?
- What is one small, realistic way I could live one of my values more intentionally this week?

5

YOUR NARRATIVES

THERE IS a story inside of you. One that you have learned to tell yourself about yourself, and about the world around you. This story has developed over time, shaped by external messages and by the meaning you have made from your experiences.

Sometimes that narrative is productive and helpful. You might believe you are capable, resilient, or powerful. Other times, the narrative becomes self-limiting, shaped by painful experiences or messages you've internalized. Over time, this narrative becomes less like a story you are telling yourself, and more like a deeply held belief.

As you continue to *align,* you will begin exploring your personal narrative with openness and curiosity. Where did it come from? Who gave it to you? Why did you believe it in the first place? Because even when the narrative appears harmful on the surface, as you dig deeper, you may find it once served a purpose for you.

As you begin this exploration, remember that narratives can be rewritten, revised, and reframed. If the story you've been telling yourself no longer makes sense, it might be time to take a more active role in shaping it. As your narrative begins to shift, you may notice that other things begin to shift along with it: your beliefs about yourself, your choices, and your outcomes.

You cannot erase the story of your past, but you *can* change how you relate to it.

Beliefs & Identity: The Story You Live Inside

There is a narrative you carry about who you are and how the world works. This story has been forming over time, beginning far earlier than you likely remember. It has been shaped by the people you've encountered, the environments you've lived in, and the experiences you've had along the way. Much of it was written long before you had the language or power to question it.

A narrative is more than just a collection of thoughts you've acquired over time. You can think of it as an organizing system your mind uses to make sense of your experiences. It takes in information, sorts it, assigns meaning, and builds a story based on the accumulation of what you've lived through. Your narrative helps answer questions like: *Who am I? What can I expect from others? What is possible for me? What can and can't happen?*

Sometimes that narrative is supportive and expansive. You might believe you are capable, resilient, or able to grow based on what you've learned about yourself or what others have reflected back to you. Other times, the narrative becomes self-limiting, shaped by painful experiences or messages you've internalized. You may come to believe that you are the outcome of what has happened to you. Sometimes, a narrative that started as something positive, or even as a strength, can change over time and become limiting.

Over time, the narrative becomes less like a story you are telling yourself and more like the reality you are living inside. It feels true not because it has been carefully examined, but because it has been repeated, reinforced, and rarely questioned.

One reason narratives feel so convincing is something called confirmation bias. This is the mind's tendency to look for, notice, and remember information that supports what you already believe, while filtering out or minimizing what contradicts it. If you believe "I'm not good enough," you may quickly notice mistakes, criticism, or rejection, while overlooking moments of success, connection, or competence. Over time, this creates a loop in which the belief feels increasingly true. Not because it is objectively accurate, but because your attention has been trained to gather evidence that supports it.

You experience reality through the lens of this narrative, through the beliefs you hold about who you are, what others are like, and what you can expect from life. These beliefs shape how you interpret events, relate to others, and understand yourself. They influence what you notice, what you dismiss, and what feels possible or impossible.

Two people can experience the same situation and walk away with completely different conclusions. For example, one person might receive feedback from a supervisor at work and think, *I'm failing. I can't do anything right. I'm never going to succeed here.* Another might interpret the same feedback as, *I'm actually starting to get this. I'm learning. Before long, I'll be able to do this confidently.* The event is the same, but the meaning is filtered through a different internal narrative.

Here's another example. One client grew up hearing they were never good enough, that an A-minus was basically an F. They learned that unless they were perfect, they were failing. Another client was raised to believe that effort mattered more than outcome, that doing your best was enough. Both entered a triathlon. One placed third in their division and felt terrible. The other finished nearly last and felt proud. Who do you think was who?

Narratives shape reality not by changing what happens, but by shaping what it *means*.

Your narrative shapes your thoughts, beliefs, and behaviors. If you believe *"I'm broken,"* you may approach life cautiously, assume things won't work out, avoid opportunities, or disengage when things become challenging, not because you lack ability, but because you expect failure. If your narrative tells you that you are unlovable, it becomes difficult to recognize or trust love when it appears. You may dismiss care, keep emotional distance, or assume people will eventually leave. If your narrative is that people can't be trusted, vulnerability may feel dangerous, and connection may remain limited even when you want it.

This process doesn't just apply to organization or habits. It shows up in how you approach relationships, work, boundaries, and self-worth. If your narrative is, *"I'm bad at relationships,"* you may withdraw early or tolerate unhealthy dynamics because you believe you don't deserve anything better. If your narrative is, *"I'm not disciplined,"* you may avoid starting anything that requires consistency. Why bother? You're not going to follow through anyway. In each case, the behavior appears to confirm the belief. It reinforces the story you've been telling yourself all along.

In clinical work, this often shows up in surprisingly ordinary ways. For example, a client once described herself as a "messy person." Her home felt chaotic and disorganized, and she saw this as clear evidence of a fixed trait. Dishes piled up. Clothes lived anywhere but the closet. The bathroom felt perpetually unmanageable. Each unfinished task reinforced the same conclusion: *This is just who I am.*

When asked what the opposite of "messy" looked like, she described someone tidy and organized. The goal wasn't to suddenly become that person overnight, but to gently revise the narrative. Instead of "I am a messy person," she began experimenting with the idea: *I am a tidy and organized person who used to be messy.*

That subtle shift made a difference. It created space for behavior to change without demanding perfection. In small moments, holding a dish, dropping clothes on the floor, she learned to pause and ask, *"What would a tidy and organized person do right now?"* Sometimes the answer was to put the dish in the sink. Sometimes it wasn't. But each small, aligned action became new evidence. Over time, the behavior changed, and so did the belief.

How Narratives Are Formed

Beliefs don't appear out of nowhere. They are formed gradually, shaped by early experiences, cultural messages, relationships, and repeated outcomes. Childhood conditioning plays a significant role, as do cultural narratives about success, worth, gender, productivity, and belonging. Past successes and failures reinforce conclusions about who you are and what you can expect. Authority figures, peers, and social environments contribute as well, offering messages that are absorbed long before they're questioned.

Early environments often assign roles: the responsible one, the quiet one, the achiever, the difficult one. These roles can become identity labels that persist long after the environment has changed. This reflects a core idea in family systems theory, which suggests that individuals develop roles within a family system to maintain balance or stability. Over time, those roles can become internalized as identity, even when they are no longer accurate or helpful.

Cultural and social messaging also play a role. Messages about success, worth, gender, productivity, and belonging shape how you see yourself. What you see and hear influences what you think, and over time, those thoughts become beliefs.

For example, imagine being in a friend group where a few people always seem effortlessly attractive. Styled, polished, and put together. Over time, it's easy to start comparing yourself, even if no one says anything out loud. You might begin to see yourself as the one who doesn't quite measure up. Less polished. Less put together. Not enough in some way. The narrative becomes: *I'm not attractive.*

But that same story could be told differently.

What if what you're comparing yourself to is just one version of attractiveness? What if your version is more subtle, but just as real? Your ease. Your presence. The way people feel comfortable around you. The fact that you can get out the door in ten minutes and go live your life. The energy you put into things that hold meaning for you. Those things count! They just don't always get the same attention.

The facts haven't changed. The meaning has.

For some people, these beliefs are tied to much deeper pain. Another client carried the belief *"I'm broken,"* rooted in a history of childhood neglect, abuse, and trauma. Substance use and self-loathing became ways of coping with that belief; not because she lacked strength, but because the story she lived inside left little room for hope or agency.

As her work progressed, the belief itself became the focus. "Broken" began to give way to a different, more accurate interpretation: *strong.* Strong for surviving. Strong for adapting. Strong for still wanting something better. That shift didn't erase her past, but it changed how she related to it. Revising the belief didn't magically solve everything, but it restored a sense of control and possibility. Behavior followed. Choices shifted. Identity loosened its grip.

Many of the beliefs that cause the most distress are not loud or obvious. They are often simple, deeply held conclusions about the self or the world. Common examples include beliefs such as…

"I'm not enough."

"I always mess things up."

"I don't deserve success."

"People can't be trusted."

These beliefs don't always show up as clear, conscious thoughts. More often, they hide beneath habits and patterns: avoidance, perfectionism, people-pleasing, overworking, or chronic self-doubt. You may not hear the belief directly, but you can see its influence in what you do or do not allow yourself to try.

One way to identify limiting beliefs is to look at repetition. When the same outcomes keep occurring, it's often because the same underlying assumptions are guiding behavior. Asking questions like, *"If this keeps happening, what must I believe about myself or the world?"* can bring those assumptions into awareness. This process isn't about assigning blame. It's about understanding the internal logic your mind and nervous system have been operating under.

Sometimes the narrative you carry is grounded in real experiences. And sometimes, the story you tell yourself about yourself or the world could benefit from revision. Not all stories are true, and just because a story was learned early or repeated often does not make it fact. This is the part of *Empowerful* where you're allowed to blame your parents, your third-grade teacher, a coach, a classmate, or the neighborhood bully. I'm only half joking.

I'll never forget working with a client in her mid-50s who shared a story from fifth grade that had shaped her entire life. You might assume this was something major or obviously traumatic. It wasn't. It was subtle. But it stuck.

She described sitting in class, listening to a teacher she admired deeply. This teacher was smart, confident, and one of the few positive female role models she had at the time. When the teacher asked a question about a reading assignment, she eagerly raised her hand, excited to participate. She wanted to be seen. She wanted to get it right. When she gave her answer, it was incorrect. Not just slightly off, but wrong enough that the teacher laughed. The class laughed. At that moment, something shifted. She learned that speaking up was risky. That being wrong meant being embarrassed. That it was safer to stay quiet.

Decades later, that moment was still shaping how she moved through the world. She hesitated to share ideas at work. She avoided situations where she might be put on the spot. She held back in conversations, even when she had something valuable to say. The original moment had long since passed, but the narrative it created, "*If I speak up and I'm wrong, I'll be humiliated,*" had never been updated.

Sometimes it really was one moment, one voice, or one experience that shaped the story, and it simply never got revised.

Belief Loops and Reinforcement

Beliefs tend to operate in predictable loops.

A belief shapes a thought. That thought generates an emotional response. Emotions influence behavior. Behavior produces results and those results are then used as evidence to reinforce the original belief.

Over time, this loop becomes self-fulfilling. Confirmation bias strengthens it, directing your attention toward information that supports what you already believe and filtering out what contradicts it. Identity, in this way, is often reinforced not by truth but by repetition.

Understanding this loop is empowering.

Here is an example. A client grew up with a highly critical parent and internalized the belief: "*I always make the wrong decision.*" As an adult, this led to paralysis and avoidance of any type of decision making. Instead of choosing a direction, he would wait, avoid, or defer. When an opportunity arose to move for his career, he couldn't commit. It was in another city. He couldn't make the decision to stay or to go. Ultimately, the opportunity passed him by, and his career remained stagnant. He didn't decide to take the opportunity, and so his belief was reinforced: "*I knew I'd make the wrong decision.*"

It shows you that beliefs are not fixed truths; they are working hypotheses that can be examined and revised. But change doesn't happen through forced positivity or denial. Rewriting your narrative does not mean pretending everything is fine or replacing painful beliefs with affirmations that don't feel believable. Sustainable change requires distinguishing between what actually happened and the meaning you assigned to it.

Revising your narrative is about creating interpretations that are more accurate, more compassionate, and more useful. New beliefs are built through evidence, particularly behavioral evidence. As your actions shift, even in small ways, they create new data. Over time, that data weakens old narratives and supports new ones.

Your Narrative Loop

As you continue to *align*, you may choose to spend some time noticing the narratives that show up in your daily life. Think of this as light observation, not deep analysis (and definitely not a full-time job). The goal is to collect small pieces of evidence over time so you can begin to see your patterns more clearly.

You might start by noticing moments that stand out: a strong reaction, a familiar thought, a behavior you keep repeating, or a situation that brings up an old feeling. Then briefly note what happened. What was the situation? What thought showed up? What did you feel? What did you do next? What was the result?

This does not need to take more than a minute or two.

Over time, these small entries begin to tell a larger story. Instead of "I always do this," you may begin to notice, "I tend to do this after criticism," or "This shows up when I feel uncertain or out of control," or "I seem to return to the role I had as a child".

The first step is to begin to identify patterns. Are there situations that keep repeating? Thoughts that consistently hold you back? Places where you feel stuck, disengaged, or reactive?

Next, begin to notice the narrative itself. The story you are telling yourself. *"If this keeps happening, what might I believe about myself, other people, or the world?"*

From there, it can help to trace where the narrative came from. You might explore earlier experiences, relationships, or messages that you received that helped shape this belief. This is about understanding how the story developed so you can start to see it as something learned, rather than something inherently true about you.

Then once you've done that, you may start to gently question and examine the narrative for evidence that supports it, as well as evidence against it. It may not be true! This helps to create flexibility in your thinking about it. Maybe there is another way to think about it that feels more accurate, more compassionate and more honest.

After that, you can choose to begin revising the narrative with flexibility, authenticity, and self-empathy.

Perhaps you weren't the villain in your story after all.

Finally, you can begin to *align* your thoughts and behaviors with this new narrative.

When Narratives Become Protective

Many painful narratives begin as attempts to make sense of difficult experiences or to stay emotionally safe. A belief like *"I don't need anyone"* may develop in response to repeated disappointment or neglect. It protects against the vulnerability of connection. Other beliefs protect in ways that are less obvious, often shielding you from something deeper or more uncomfortable.

These beliefs are not random or irrational. They developed for a reason, and at some point, they likely made sense. The more useful question is whether they still fit your life now.

Narratives can be protective because they keep you with what feels known and predictable. They offer a sense of certainty. But questioning them can feel like shedding an identity, or opening the door to something more complex, more painful, or harder to face.

For example, imagine someone who believes people don't like them because they are *awkward*. That narrative becomes the explanation for every difficult interaction. It feels clear. Consistent. Settled. But it also protects them from looking deeper. From asking whether something else might be happening. It may prevent them from exploring patterns in communication, expectations in relationships, or the ways they show up with others. It may also protect them from the vulnerability of trying something different and risking rejection in a new way.

Sometimes the surface-level explanation feels easier to hold than the deeper questions underneath it. Because those questions may require introspection, behavior change, or coming to terms with something painful or uncertain.

This is how protective narratives tend to operate. They offer an explanation that feels complete, even when it isn't the full picture. They reduce uncertainty and give you something to hold onto. You might notice this in the way you explain difficult interactions or recurring patterns in your life. A single reason begins to account for everything. It feels consistent, predictable and even logical.

But if the same explanation keeps showing up, especially one that places the problem entirely on something fixed or unchangeable, it may be worth pausing to ask: *is this the full story, or just the safest one?*

A Note of Compassion Before We Move On

Some narratives are tied to deep pain. If your beliefs are rooted in trauma, neglect, abuse or harm this work should be approached gently. If it feels too triggering or difficult to do on your own, I **strongly** encourage you to reach out to a mental health professional for support, ideally one who specializes in trauma.

If you experienced trauma, I want you to know that you are the one in control of your story here. You are the one to choose what stays and what is revised. You are not expected to reinterpret painful experiences in any way that minimizes what happened to you.

The ways you learned to think, feel and respond were shaped by your experiences, whatever you endured. Be careful not invalidate your own experience, or rush yourself into alternative explanations that feel disconnected from your truth.

Revising the Narrative

Understanding your narratives is empowering, but changing them can feel uncomfortable. Letting go of a long-held narrative can feel destabilizing, even when the belief itself is painful. Familiar stories provide structure and predictability. They help you anticipate what will happen, even if those expectations are limiting.

Changing a narrative means stepping into uncertainty, because you are allowing for outcomes that don't fit the old story. Because of this, many people unconsciously return to familiar beliefs, even when they no longer serve them.

Beliefs are working hypotheses that can be examined and revised. Rewriting your narrative does not mean pretending everything is fine or replacing painful beliefs with forced positivity. It means distinguishing between what actually happened and the meaning you assigned to it. Revising your narrative is about creating interpretations that are more accurate, more compassionate, and more useful.

When I do narrative work with clients, I encourage them to approach their story with empathy. This can be surprisingly difficult. Many people find it much easier to extend compassion to others than to themselves.

Because of this, I will often ask clients to shift their perspective. If an adult client is describing their childhood or adolescence, I may ask them to imagine that the story they are telling belongs not to them, but to any child or adolescent. How would they understand what that child went through? How would they explain it? What would they feel toward that person?

More often than not, they are able to access a level of empathy and compassion that feels out of reach when they are viewing the same story as their own. The details haven't changed. Instead, the interpretation has softened.

Before You Continue

Your personal narratives are the stories you tell yourself about yourself and the world around you. They are formed through messages that you've received throughout your life. Whether you heard the message once or a thousand times, some stories become deeply held beliefs. Sometimes these beliefs are helpful and empowering. Other times, they are limiting and self-reinforcing.

As you begin to understand your story with greater context and clarity, something becomes possible: you can choose how you relate to it. You may decide to revise parts of it if they no longer serve you.

Sometimes, you may even realize that parts of the story were never entirely true in the first place.

I love when clients have that "aha!" moment, when they realize they are not their story. Like tall tales, the narrative may be exaggerated or distorted. Like fables, there may be a lesson there, just not necessarily the one you first learned.

I'm hopeful that you are feeling even more *Empowerful* at this point, with a clear process to begin identifying and changing your narratives. You were invited to start exploring your narrative loop by noticing patterns, identifying the story itself, exploring where it came from, questioning the evidence that supports it, and experimenting with more accurate and compassionate interpretations.

You don't have to keep living inside a story that no longer fits.

Pause and Reflect

Take a moment to pause and reflect, without trying to fix or solve anything yet.

- What narratives do you want to challenge and change?
- What patterns in your life feel repetitive or stuck?
- Who told you something about yourself that you once believed but no longer do?
- What evidence have you been using to support this story—and what evidence have you been ignoring?
- If this narrative were no longer true, what might you allow yourself to do differently?

6

YOUR THOUGHTS

In my work, I frequently see people assume that their thoughts are facts.

I mean… why wouldn't they be? You thought it, right? So it must be true.

And yet, when we slow down and examine those thoughts more closely, that often isn't the case. While some thoughts are valid and grounded in reality, others can be questioned, challenged, reframed, and reconsidered.

There are certain patterns of thinking that tend to create a significant amount of distress. They are so common and recognizable that they've actually been categorized and studied. Psychotherapists are trained to notice them in the therapy room, and they also exist "out in the wild", because they show up everywhere.

These patterns are part of an evidence-based approach called Cognitive Behavioral Therapy, or CBT. At its core, CBT helps people recognize how their thoughts influence their feelings, and how those feelings drive behavior. When thoughts are distorted or unhelpful, the emotional and behavioral consequences often follow.

In practice, I often help clients slow things down and "find the thought." That's how our CBT work begins.

Sometimes we start with a behavior and work backward. Other times we begin with a feeling or a noticeable shift in mood. And sometimes the thought is right there, front and center. There isn't just one way in, but there is almost always a way to trace it back.

Understanding your thoughts is incredibly useful in a practical, everyday way. Most people experience a near-constant stream of internal dialogue, which is a running commentary that shapes how they interpret themselves and the world around them. (And yes, I know there are some people who don't have that constant chatter… but most of the people I work with definitely do.)

If that internal voice is distorted, overly critical, or disconnected from reality, it's going to impact how you feel and how you function. Which is why learning to notice and work with your thoughts can be so helpful.

Sometimes it helps to think of thoughts like clouds in the sky. They move. They shift. They change. They come and go. You can observe them without getting attached to them. And just because a thought appears doesn't mean it's true, needs your attention, or is permanent.

Even the uncomfortable ones pass.

Your Thinking Affects You

Thoughts play a powerful role. How you experience yourself and the world around you is shaped, in large part, by how you think about it. Your feelings don't occur at random; they are the responses to your thoughts. When the way you think shifts, the way you feel often shifts too.

This does **not** mean you can simply "think better" and poof! magically feel better. (If only.) It means that the thoughts you have play a powerful role in shaping your emotional experience, especially the ones that happen quickly and automatically. Learning to notice and work with those thoughts gives you more influence over how you feel and how you respond.

One of the most useful ideas to understand is this: **thoughts are not facts.** They can feel like facts. They can sound like facts. They can behave like overconfident people in the comments section of anything on the internet. Still not facts.

They can be explored, questioned, challenged, and reframed. Remember that just because a thought appears quickly, or feels convincing, that doesn't mean it's accurate, helpful, or even true.

Thoughts, Feelings, and Behavior: The Basic Loop

Some of you will already be familiar with Cognitive Behavioral Therapy, or CBT for short. Many therapists specialize in this approach, myself included. CBT is a widely used, evidence-based form of psychotherapy built on a simple but powerful idea: **thoughts, feelings, and behaviors are connected.**

What you think influences how you feel. How you feel influences what you do. Sometimes the behaviors that follow are adaptive and helpful. Other times, they're reactive, avoidant, or self-defeating. The goal of CBT is to help you understand the pattern and respond differently if what's happening isn't working for you, or is creating unnecessary distress.

CBT focuses on helping people notice the relationship between:

- What they think.
- How they feel.
- How they act.

Rather than assuming situations alone cause distress, CBT looks at how interpretations, beliefs, and learned responses shape emotional reactions. Many of these patterns develop over time, often as understandable responses to past experiences. CBT brings these patterns into awareness so they can be examined, tested, and adjusted when they're no longer working.

It works because it's practical, collaborative, and skills-based. You learn how to challenge unhelpful thoughts, experiment with new behaviors, and respond in more balanced ways. With practice, your brain starts to form new pathways. Over time, distress decreases, clarity increases, and functioning improves.

When the Connection Is Obvious and When It's Not

Sometimes the thought–feeling–behavior connection is obvious. You think something, feel something, and act accordingly. Other times, it's much less clear, and this is where people may feel confused. You may notice a sudden shift in mood without knowing why. You were having a great day, and now you feel anxious, overwhelmed, or hopeless.

What happened?

Often, it helps to work **backward** from the feeling to the thought.

Maybe you saw something.

Maybe you said something to yourself without fully noticing it.

Maybe there was no obvious trigger at all.

For example, you might be sitting at your computer when a thought pops up:

"I'm drowning in work. I'm never going to finish all of this."

That thought creates a feeling of overwhelm. Feeling overwhelmed leads to avoidance, shutting down, or frantic overworking. The thought came first, even if you didn't notice it at the time.

If you back up even further, maybe it started with an email from that one particularly demanding member of your team hitting your inbox. You went from "Bing!", receiving the notification, to tearing up and questioning every decision you've ever made in life… without actually knowing what the heck just happened.

When you slow it down, what felt like one overwhelming moment was actually a rapid sequence: situation → thought → feeling →

behavior. It all happened in seconds, but it took you from having a good day to shutdown mode.

One client I worked with felt intense anxiety in a long-distance relationship. His partner usually sent a goodnight text, but occasionally forgot. When that happened, his mind filled in the blanks.

He must be with someone else. That's why he didn't text.

Once that thought appeared, his brain went into confirmation mode, scanning for "evidence" to support it. The anxiety escalated quickly. To relieve the discomfort, he began obsessively texting his partner, sometimes accusing him of cheating. Predictably, this led to conflict and strain in the relationship.

The anxiety wasn't random.

It was driven by distorted thinking.

Through CBT work, he began to recognize the patterns underneath the distress: jumping to conclusions, catastrophizing, and disqualifying the positive aspects of the relationship that clearly supported commitment and trust. When he learned to challenge those thoughts, not by forcing positivity, but by checking for accuracy, his emotional response changed. And once the feeling changed, the behavior followed.

Thoughts influence feelings. Feelings influence behavior. Sometimes the thought needs attention first. Sometimes the behavior does. And learning to slow down this process, to notice what's happening between stimulus and response, is one of the most powerful skills you can develop.

How This Plays Out in Real Life

- A **thought** appears (often automatically).
- That thought creates a **feeling.**
- The feeling drives a **behavior.**
- The behavior leads to an **outcome.**
- The outcome then **reinforces the original thought.**

Over time, this loop can become so familiar that it runs in the background without conscious awareness.

The work of CBT is not about stopping thoughts or emotions; it's about **interrupting the loop**:

- Questioning the thought.
- Tolerating the feeling.
- Choosing a different behavior.

When even one part of the loop changes, the entire pattern can shift.

If you look at the loop, you might notice something: the thought comes first.

But most people don't experience it that way.

They notice the feeling.

You wake up anxious.

You feel suddenly irritated.

Your mood drops out of nowhere.

Your chest tightens, your energy crashes, your patience disappears.

And the question becomes: *Why do I feel like this?*

Often, the answer isn't obvious because the thought that started the loop happened so quickly that you didn't even register it.

This is where **automatic thoughts** come in.

Automatic Thoughts: What Happens Behind the Scenes

Many of the thoughts that affect us the most happen automatically, often in a split second, outside of conscious awareness. You might go from feeling calm or content to anxious, irritated, or discouraged without knowing why. But something *did* happen. A thought occurred.

This process is called **automaticity**.

It happens fast, sometimes in a fraction of a second. You can go from feeling happy to seeing something in your environment to feeling anxious almost instantly.

Imagine this scenario: you once went through a painful breakup with someone who had unpredictable anger. That person drove a yellow car. One day, you're driving along, enjoying music, feeling fine, and suddenly you feel anxious, maybe even panicked. What happened? A yellow car happened. Without conscious awareness, you noticed a yellow car pull out into traffic. A thought flashed through your mind: *"Is that my ex?"* And before you could reason through it, your body reacted. Fear set in. Your heart raced. You went from enjoying the moment to feeling unsafe, within seconds.

That's automaticity.

Understanding automaticity helps explain why emotions can change before we can name a reason, and why slowing down to notice these patterns can create space for choice rather than reaction.

Automatic thoughts operate behind the scenes. They're shaped by past experiences, beliefs, and learned patterns, and they tend to follow well-worn neural pathways. The brain is efficient. Once a pathway has been used repeatedly, like *yellow car equals fear*, it becomes easier and faster to travel it again. This is why the same emotional reactions can show up again and again, even when circumstances have changed.

By adulthood, many of these patterns are deeply established. External influences and internal experiences have worked together over time to create familiar loops of thinking and feeling. Changing them takes conscious effort, awareness, and repetition - but it's possible.

Why the Brain Distorts

Way back when, your primal brain had one very important job: **don't get eaten**.

It was responsible for keeping you safe from truly terrifying threats, woolly mammoths, saber-toothed tigers, mysterious rustling in the bushes while you were out hunting, gathering, or attempting to make fire without burning everything down.

Your brain was on high alert at all times, scanning the environment for danger and signaling you quickly if something felt even remotely off. That system was incredibly useful. If your brain hesitated to analyze whether the growl you heard was *really* a threat, you didn't survive long enough to pass on your genes.

Fast forward to modern life. The mammoths are gone. The tigers are not lurking behind your car. But your brain? It's still running the same software.

There are a few different ways the brain distorts thoughts, and it does this for a reason. Your brain is not designed to make you happy, fulfilled, or emotionally regulated. **It is designed to keep you safe.** And it will always prioritize safety over accuracy, comfort, or joy.

To do this efficiently, the brain relies on shortcuts. These shortcuts help it respond quickly, but they can also distort perception. Some of the most common ways this shows up include:

- **Negativity bias**, which causes the brain to focus more on potential problems than neutral or positive information.
- **Threat detection**, which prioritizes scanning for danger, rejection, or loss (even in places where none exists).
- **Pattern recognition**, where the brain fills in gaps based on past experience rather than present evidence.
- **Emotional reasoning**, where feelings are treated as facts ("I feel anxious, so something must be wrong").

These tendencies were incredibly useful for survival when danger was physical and immediate. In modern life, however, they often show up in board meetings, relationships, text messages, and late-night overthinking. Instead of protecting you from predators, they can create unnecessary anxiety, self-doubt, and emotional distress.

The key takeaway here is that your brain is **very good at doing the job it evolved to do.** The work now is learning when that system is helpful… and when it's reacting (or overreacting) to threats that no longer exist.

Common Cognitive Distortions

One of my favorite moments in therapy is when we begin talking about cognitive distortions. It's often a rapport-building moment, because clients realize I'm also an imperfect human.

The first time I learned about cognitive distortions, I was in Social Work 101. They were neatly packaged in a list, and I remember thinking, *"Uh oh. Uh oh. I do that. And that. And that. And that."* Thankfully, I learned that **we all** have distorted thinking at times. It's only when these patterns show up frequently or intensely that they begin to create distress or interfere with functioning.

Cognitive distortions are habitual ways of thinking that can skew perception and intensify emotional reactions. They are patterns your mind falls into automatically, especially when you're stressed, overwhelmed, or emotionally activated.

Many of these thinking patterns develop for a reason; they are attempts to make sense of situations quickly, predict outcomes, or protect you from discomfort. The problem is that they often fill in gaps with assumptions, amplify the negative, or ignore relevant context, which can intensify how you feel and influence what you do next.

Some of the most common include:

- **All-or-Nothing Thinking**
- Seeing things in absolutes, such as *"always," "never,"* or *"every time."*
- **Magnification and Minimization**

- Exaggerating the importance of problems or minimizing your strengths, successes, or positive experiences.
- **Catastrophizing**
- Assuming the worst possible outcome and focusing only on what could go wrong.
- **Mind Reading**
- Assuming you know what others are thinking without clear evidence.
- **Personalization**
- Taking responsibility for events or outcomes that are outside your control.
- **Jumping to Conclusions**
- Assigning meaning or intent without enough information to support it.
- **Magical Thinking**
- Believing that certain thoughts or actions will influence unrelated outcomes.
- **Overgeneralization**
- Drawing broad conclusions based on a single event or limited experience.
- **Emotional Reasoning**
- Treating feelings as facts: *"I feel this way, so it must be true."*
- **"Should" Statements**
- Rigid expectations about yourself or others, based on beliefs about how things *should* be.
- **Confirmation Bias**
- Noticing or remembering only the information that supports existing beliefs.
- **Filtering or Disqualifying the Positive**
- Focusing on negatives while overlooking or dismissing positive experiences.

Just a Quick Note on the "Shoulds"

In my opinion, "should" statements are one of the most problematic cognitive distortions. They're subtle, persuasive, and often masquerade as motivation or good intentions. In reality, they can trap you into believing all kinds of inauthentic things about yourself and the world around you.

"Shoulds" tell you who you're supposed to be, how you're supposed to feel, what you're supposed to think, and how you're supposed to act. They create an internal rulebook that often has very little to do with who you actually are or what you genuinely need. When followed unquestioned, these rules tend to lead to chronic self-criticism, pressure, and a persistent sense that you're falling short, even when you're doing quite well.

They thrive on repetition.

You should be more disciplined.

You should be easier going.

You should want to do this.

You should be able to handle that.

Over time, these messages start to feel less like thoughts and more like facts.

Conversely, "shoulds" are just as powerful when they tell you who or what you *shouldn't* be. They police your emotions, interests, needs, and limits. You shouldn't feel angry. You shouldn't need help. You shouldn't care so much. You shouldn't want more. Over time, these rules disconnect you from your authentic self and teach you to override internal signals in order to appear acceptable, capable, or "together."

Many "shoulds" are inherited rather than chosen. They come from family expectations, cultural norms, professional roles, social comparison, and increasingly from the curated versions of life we see online. They can sound like: You should have figured your career out by now. You should put your family first. You should be able to handle this on your own. You should be grateful and not complain. You should be more productive. You should want to have children. (I know many of you felt that last one.)

These messages are often absorbed early on and reinforced over time, until they feel like truth instead of influence.

Social media is particularly effective at convincing us there is a *right* way to do things: the right aesthetic, the right timing, the right amount of ease. And if we can't do it *that* way, we often don't do it at all. Suddenly, real life feels like it's not measuring up to something that was staged, filtered, and posted in under sixty seconds.

This is where perfectionism often enters the picture.

Perfectionism is often misunderstood as a strength, but clinically, it's usually a rigid set of rules about how things *must* be done in order to be acceptable. It tends to show up as all-or-nothing thinking, which is also a cognitive distortion, and says: if it can't be done perfectly it's not worth doing at all. It raises the bar so high that starting feels overwhelming, and finishing feels impossible. Underneath perfectionism is often a fear of making mistakes, being judged, feeling like an imposter, or not being *enough*. Ironically, instead of helping you do things better, perfectionism often keeps you from doing them at all

I worked with a client who eventually realized that perfectionism wasn't a strength — it was a barrier. She believed she *should* only start tasks when the timing was right, the process was clear, and the conditions were ideal. In practice, that meant she rarely started. Fear of doing it "wrong" kept her stuck. When she shifted her mindset to **action over perfection**, something changed. Action didn't have to look polished or impressive; it just had to happen.

Another client needed to complete continuing education hours for her job. Her perfectionistic tendencies told her that "doing it right" meant blocking off several uninterrupted hours, sitting at a desk, taking detailed notes, and fully focusing. Because her life didn't realistically allow for that, she kept putting it off, and the pressure mounted. Once she reframed action over perfection, the solution became obvious. She listened to the lectures while walking her dog. The credits got completed. The task got done. And perhaps most importantly, the internal tension around it dissolved.

I see this same pattern in goal-setting, too. One client wanted to map out goals for the year but felt completely stuck. In her mind, the process *should* involve a weekend away with her partner, a beautiful planner, and a calm, inspired mindset. Because real life didn't match that image, she couldn't begin. In reality, aligned action looked like sitting at the kitchen table together, using printer paper, and eating frozen pizza. Once she let go of the "should," she could actually start.

Another realized she wasn't a "go with the flow" kind of person; she was a "plan it" kind of person. For years, she had been telling herself she *should* be more spontaneous, more flexible, more easygoing. That belief created constant friction. When friends invited her to do things at the last minute, she would either say yes and feel resentful or say no and feel guilty. Once she stopped trying to be the person she thought she should be and allowed herself to be who she actually was, her internal narrative shifted. She felt more confident saying no when she needed to. She felt calmer about her decisions. The guilt softened, not because she became less caring, but because her choices were finally aligned.

A useful reframe is this: **values tend to feel grounding and clarifying; "shoulds" tend to feel pressurized and forced.** Values invite you into alignment. "Shoulds" push you toward being someone you're not. An excellent question to ask yourself is: **Am I trying to be the person I think I should be or the person I really am?**

Creating New Thought Patterns

Because thoughts move quickly and follow established neural pathways, people often ask: *Will I ever be able to do this automatically?*

After I introduce CBT to clients—after we've talked about how thoughts connect to feelings and feelings connect to behaviors, and we've walked through real-life examples together—this is one of the most common questions I get. *Will I be able to do this on my own? Will it ever happen automatically?*

The answer is yes, but it takes practice.

It won't happen immediately, and that's part of the process. Sometimes I'll ask clients, *How long have you been thinking this way?* Some will say, "All my life." Others will say, "Years." That becomes a meaningful moment in the conversation, because if you've been traveling down the same mental pathway for years, it is well-worn. It's efficient. It's automatic. Now you are creating a brand new path in your brain. And just like any new skill, any new ability, it requires intention at the beginning. It takes effort. It takes repetition.

Over time, with practice, it becomes more natural. Eventually, it can become automatic, just like the old patterns once were.

At first, noticing and challenging distorted thoughts requires conscious effort. That is one of the first assignments I give to clients once they identify a particular thought or pattern of thinking that creates distress. The assignment is to notice when their mood changes, and then back into exactly what they were thinking just before the noticeable shift in mood.

Over time, as new ways of thinking are practiced and reinforced, new neural pathways form. Eventually, more balanced thoughts can arise more quickly, sometimes even automatically. This doesn't mean you'll never have distorted thoughts again. It means you'll become better at recognizing them, and challenging them, or reframing them when appropriate.

When you consistently and intentionally change how you think, you begin to feel differently. And when you feel differently, your behavior often follows.

How to Start: The Basic CBT Process

When I first introduce this work to clients, I keep it simple.

Below is a process you can begin to use in your daily life to start to identify and challenge problematic thought patterns. It may feel a little slow or intentional at first, but with practice, it becomes more natural and eventually automatic.

First, notice the shift.

Something changes in your mood. You feel anxious, irritated, discouraged, overwhelmed. That shift is your cue to pause and explore.

Second, identify the thought.

Ask yourself: *What just went through my mind? What was I thinking about?* Even if it feels fast or unclear, try to capture the first thing that comes up, and be as specific as possible when you identify the thought. It might be something like:

"I can't handle this."

"They're upset with me."

"I'm going to mess this up."

And if the thought isn't obvious right away, that's okay. Sometimes it's easier to start with the feeling and work backward.

Third, name the feeling.

Put words to the emotional response.

In my experience, identifying feelings can be challenging and takes practice, along with expanding your "feelings vocabulary." I often use a "feelings wheel" with clients. Feel free to look it up!

Part of the difficulty is that many people default to broad, blanket emotions: angry, sad, happy, guilty - or the one no partner, spouse, or friend wants to hear… *"I'm fine."*

You might say "angry," when you actually feel irritated, frustrated, agitated, or enraged.

You might say "sad," when you feel lonely, hurt, disappointed, or discouraged.

You might say "anxious," when you feel worried, panicked, inadequate, or uncertain.

You might say "happy," when you mean proud, hopeful, relieved, or content.

The more specific you can be, the more clarity you gain.

Fourth, notice the behavior.

What do you do next?

Did you withdraw? Shut down? Get defensive? Overexplain? Avoid? Reach for your phone, a snack, or a distraction?

This part is key, because behavior is often the outward expression of what's happening internally, and it's also what keeps the existing loop going.

Fifth, examine the thought.

Do this with curiosity, not criticism.

Begin to gently question the thought: Is this 100% true? What evidence supports this? What evidence might not support it? Am I jumping to conclusions? What might someone else think about this situation?

Sixth, create a more balanced thought.

If the thought is distorted or creating distress, the goal isn't to "fix" it with forced positivity or pretend everything is fine. Instead, try to shift it into something more balanced and realistic.

Not a forced positive thought. Not "everything is amazing."

A balanced thought usually lives somewhere in the middle, because it acknowledges what's difficult, while also making space for what might still be true. It's validating *and* flexible.

For example, instead of "I always mess things up," you might land on, "I made a mistake this time, but that doesn't mean I always do."

The key is that it feels believable to you.

Something more realistic and helpful, like:

"This is hard, but I can take it one step at a time."

"I don't actually know what they're thinking."

"I've handled things like this before."

And finally, notice what changes.

Sometimes the feeling softens. Sometimes it doesn't fully go away, but it becomes more manageable. You may also notice a shift in your behavior. You respond instead of react. You pause instead of spiral. You choose something different, even in a small way.

A few Examples

Let's walk through a few quick examples.

Example 1: The Email

You receive an email from your boss.

Shift: You feel a sudden wave of anxiety.

Thought: "I must have done something wrong."

Feeling: Anxiety (more worry than fear)

Behavior: You start overthinking, reviewing your work, maybe asking coworkers if they've heard anything.

Now, pause and examine the thought:

Is this a fact? No.

What evidence supports it? Not much.

What evidence doesn't support it? You recently received positive feedback. Nothing has indicated a problem.

Balanced thought: "I don't have enough information yet. This could be completely neutral."

What changes: The anxiety softens. You're able to open the email without spiraling.

Example 2: The Text Message

You text a friend. They don't respond.

Shift: Your mood drops.

Thought: "They're ignoring me."

Feeling: Hurt, maybe a little rejected

Behavior: You check your phone repeatedly, consider sending another message, or start withdrawing.

Now, examine the thought:

Is this 100% true? No.

What are other possibilities? They're busy. They forgot. They haven't seen it yet.

Balanced thought: "I don't actually know why they haven't responded yet."

What changes: The emotional intensity decreases. You're less likely to react impulsively or assume the worst.

Example 3: The To-Do List

You look at everything you need to get done.

Shift: You feel overwhelmed.

Thought: "I'm never going to get all of this done."

Feeling: Overwhelm

Behavior: You avoid starting, scroll your phone, or shut down.

Now, examine the thought:

Is this completely accurate? Not really—it's all-or-nothing thinking.

Is it helpful? No.

Balanced thought: "I don't need to do everything right now. I can start with one thing."

What changes: The overwhelm becomes more manageable. You're able to begin, even in a small way.

The CBT Process: Quick Reference

If you want a quick way to remember this process, here it is:

1. **Notice the Shift**
2. Something changed in your mood.
3. **Identify the Thought**
4. What just went through my mind?
5. **Name the Feeling**
6. What am I actually feeling?
7. **Notice the Behavior**
8. What did I do next?
9. **Examine the Thought**
10. Is this true? What's the evidence?
11. **Create a Balanced Thought**
12. What's a more realistic way to see this?
13. **Notice What Changes**
14. What feels or looks different now?

Why This Works

Every time you slow down to explore your thinking and consciously decide to reframe or challenge a thought, you interrupt an automatic loop that may not be working for you anymore. CBT work isn't about controlling your thoughts or policing your mind, because thoughts arise automatically, and there isn't a reliable way to stop them from forming in the first place. If there were, I would be a very rich and famous therapist (and probably retired by now). Instead, the work is about what you do when those thoughts show up, and how you respond to them.

Every time you create a more balanced thought, you begin building a new pathway. Every time you respond differently, you reinforce it.

People often assume they are controlled by their thoughts, but that's not actually true. You may not be able to control what shows up, but you *can* control what you do with it. **That distinction is powerful, because each time you respond differently, you create new evidence.** By pairing insight with action you are showing yourself, in real time, that another version is possible.

This is also why repetition is essential. You've practiced thinking, feeling, and responding in a particular way for a long time, so it makes sense that it feels automatic. So it also makes sense that changing your thinking doesn't happen all at once. This is going to be a gradual process.

If the skeptical part of you is wondering: *"How is doing this once or twice going to make a difference?"* the answer is actually quite simple: it works because you are consciously doing something differently. And when you do something differently, by interrupting a pattern, you are creating the possibility for a different outcome.

You can't change something you don't acknowledge, but once you identify the thought, understand the feeling, and notice the behavior that follows, you are no longer operating on autopilot! You're practicing a skill that is structured, repeatable, and applicable in real situations - with real outcomes.

Over time, this cognitive shift can reduce emotional distress and lead to healthier, more intentional choices. You can begin to shift *how* you think and in doing so, improve how you feel and what you choose to do. That's how change happens! Not all at once, but in small repeated actions over time.

Before You Continue

Thoughts are not facts. They can be questioned, challenged, and changed.

Cognitive Behavioral Therapy offers a framework you can use to understand the relationship between your thoughts, feelings, and behaviors. When you begin to see how these pieces interact, you also begin to see where change is possible.

There are many common cognitive distortions. These are patterns of thinking that influence how you feel. In their more extreme or persistent forms, they can create significant distress. Learning to recognize these patterns is one of the first steps toward changing them.

We also explored how automatic thoughts happen beneath the surface, often so quickly that you don't even realize they're there. With curiosity, awareness, and practice, you can begin to slow down that process. And in that space, something shifts: you gain the ability to choose a different way of thinking. The initial goal is not perfection. It's to begin finding flexibility in your thinking.

Flexible thinking allows you to consider alternative perspectives, respond more intentionally, and reduce unnecessary distress. It creates room for more accurate, balanced, and helpful thoughts—ones that actually support how you want to live. What you've learned here is immediately usable. My hope is that you begin to apply these tools in real-life situations as they happen out there "in the wild," as I say to my clients. And again, not perfectly, but intentionally.

Over time, you'll start to recognize patterns more quickly. You'll interrupt them more easily. And with practice, what once felt effortful may begin to feel more natural.

One client said it really well: "I have to be intentional about how much I give to these thoughts. I have to be the one to decide."

I hope you'll take a moment to reflect back on everything you've accomplished in *Part II: Align*. You've identified your values. Your internal compass for how you want to live. You've explored the narratives shaped by your experiences and begun to question which ones still serve you. You've started to understand how your thoughts influence your emotions and shape your behavior.

And now, it's time to *do something* with all of it!

Pause and Reflect

Take a moment to pause and reflect, without trying to fix or solve anything yet.

- Which cognitive distortions do you recognize in your own thinking?
- Are there certain thoughts that show up repeatedly when you feel anxious, overwhelmed, or discouraged?
- Are there any "should" statements that feel particularly loud or persistent?
- What is one thought you've had recently that might not be entirely true, even if it felt convincing in the moment?

PART III

ACTIVATE

Your Readiness • Your Activation • Your Change

In the first part of *Empowerful*, you assessed where you are: your body, your world, and your capacity. In the second, you began aligning your inner world by identifying your values, examining your narratives, and learning to work more intentionally with your thoughts.

Now it is time to activate.

This is where insight begins to turn into action. Not rushed action. Not performative action. Meaningful action that fits who you are, what you've learned, and what your real life can support.

Take a moment to notice what you've already accomplished. You completed a thorough assessment of yourself. You explored what you care about most and clarified your core values. You examined the narratives you've been living inside, and began deciding which ones still make sense. You learned how to recognize and challenge unhelpful thought patterns.

You did all of that with curiosity and openness.

And I want you to notice something else. The way I'm talking to you right now is intentional. I'm speaking to you as someone who is capable of change. I'm reminding you of what you've already done so that you can recognize your own ability to do what comes next.

In this final part, *Activate*, you'll begin putting everything together. First, we'll explore readiness and the process of change so you can understand where you are and what may be getting in the way. Then we'll focus on activation, translating everything you now understand about yourself into meaningful action that fits your real life. Finally, we'll look at change itself: how it unfolds, how to stay engaged with it, and how to keep going when things don't go perfectly.

Change does not happen all at once. It happens through small, repeated actions over time.

Each time you follow through, even in a small way, you strengthen your sense of agency. Confidence does not come from waiting until you feel fully ready. It grows as a result of doing something. Action builds momentum. Momentum reshapes habits. And over time, those habits help create a life that looks and feels different.

Now it is time to take everything you've learned and move forward feeling **empowerful**.

7

YOUR READINESS

By this point in *Empowerful*, you've done a great deal of meaningful work. You've assessed where you are, aligned with what matters most, and you're getting ready to take action.

But before you dive in headfirst, pause and ask yourself: **Are you actually ready for change?**

This may sound like a simple question, but readiness is more nuanced than people often realize. Many people assume that wanting change should be enough. They believe change will begin to occur when they are motivated, eager, frustrated, uncomfortable or just……fed up!

But that is not always how change works.

Readiness is not always an all-or-nothing state; it can exist on a spectrum as well, and can shift over time. It sounds like: S*omething needs to be different, and I'm willing to try.* That doesn't require perfect conditions. It requires enough willingness, support, and intention to begin.

Readiness is about being willing to take a step despite uncertainty. It reflects a point where awareness, motivation, and capacity have aligned *enough* to support movement, even if things still feel imperfect or unclear.

By now you've gained some clarity, and have a good idea of where you'd like to go with it. So the question becomes not only *What do I want to change?* but also *Where am I in the process of changing it?*

Why Wanting Change Isn't Enough

Change is a fascinating process. It's also far more nuanced than most people realize.

People often ask why do people change, or when will someone change. The answer is rarely simple. Change can happen in an instant, sparked by a single insight or moment, or it can unfold slowly, over time, through awareness, intention, and repeated attempts.

At its core, change is not a single decision or action. It is a process.

In my clinical work, I often take time to explain the stages of change to clients because I've found this framework to be incredibly grounding. Not because everyone follows it perfectly, which they don't, but because it gives language to something that often feels confusing and nonlinear. It helps people understand where they are, why they might feel stuck, and what kind of step actually makes sense next.

The Stages of Change

At its core, the stages of change describe how people move toward meaningful, lasting change.

The first stage is **denial**. In this stage, a person may not recognize that there is a problem at all. Even when there is chaos, conflict, or negative consequences, they may feel confused, defensive, or unable to clearly identify what's wrong. They may minimize the issue, explain it away, or feel baffled about why others are concerned. Even when there are consequences, the problem may still feel unclear, exaggerated, or unrelated to their own behavior.

When someone is in this stage, there is not yet enough awareness, ownership, or discomfort for change to begin. Sometimes this is because the person genuinely cannot see the pattern yet. Other times, denial functions as protection. If seeing the truth would bring shame, fear, grief, or overwhelm, the mind may keep the problem at a distance.

I might hear a lot of minimization of consequences, deflection of concerns, defensiveness, and blaming others for problems. My goal in this stage isn't confrontation or forcing any type of insight. My job is to gently begin to increase their awareness using open-ended questions, reflecting patterns I might observe, explore consequences in a nonjudgmental way, and help someone to see discrepancies between what they want and what is currently happening.

Next is **precontemplation**, where a person begins to sense that *something* isn't working. They may not be able to name it yet, but there's a growing awareness that something feels off. They may sense dissatisfaction, discomfort, or repeated problems, but not yet have a clear understanding of the issue or their role in it.

A person in this stage will often feel foggy, unclear, but because they are no longer fully disconnected from the problem, they are beginning to notice patterns, describe symptoms or issues without clearly identifying causes, sense that change may be needed, but not yet know where to begin. They may seek help, but are confused about what type of support they need.

My role here is to begin to help someone to identify patterns, slow down and organize thoughts and feelings that are confusing, explore what they believe is happening, and ask questions that help someone begin to link symptoms to thoughts, behaviors and context. They begin to name the actual issue with more clarity.

Contemplation follows. This is often a stage of ambivalence. A person recognizes that change may be needed, but feels unsure, hesitant, or conflicted. They may not yet understand what exactly needs to change, or they may feel torn between the discomfort of staying the same and the uncertainty of doing something different.

When someone is contemplating change, they're experiencing ambivalence. I might hear someone expressing the pros and cons of doing something or not doing something, they might be debating whether or not something makes sense, or they are exploring multiple sides of an issue. They can see reasons to change, or do something differently, but they're still really hesitant. There's apprehension, there's waffling.

Ambivalence isn't resistance, it's a normal part of change when someone isn't exactly sure what to do or how to go about it yet, but they are aware there's a problem.

My role when a client is contemplating change is to help them identify what might tip their decisional balance. I might help to evoke reasons for change, and the risks of staying the same. I might help them to explore the pros and cons of change versus staying the same. I might help to clarify values, by asking the question "What would you want your choices to reflect?" I may also normalize their hesitation, approach with curiosity, and help to build some motivation and momentum without pressure. I realize I've used the word curiosity a lot in this book, but curiosity implies taking a look at something to learn more about it, to see it for what it is without judgment.

Then comes **preparation**. This is where insight sharpens. A person begins to understand what's happening, how they might be contributing to it, and that change is possible. They start considering options, gathering information, and imagining what doing things differently might look like. They're shifting from thinking to planning.

Preparation occurs when someone has decided to change their behavior or make a change in their life and they begin to think about how they can do this. During this stage they're going to make minor changes or change small things to support the goal but they might not completely go all in.

My role here is to help someone determine the best course of action. I might help them to develop a plan. I might help them to identify small, achievable tasks that lead towards the bigger solution. I might help them break things down into small, manageable steps. Perhaps we identify barriers and problem-solve for them ahead of time. We might address perfectionism, or fear of failure. Then I reinforce self efficacy and support building confidence. This is the "You can do this!" phase.

Action is the stage where people begin taking clear, concrete steps toward change. It's common for people to move back and forth between preparation and action. Someone might try a small change, realize it's not the right approach, and return to preparation. Additional information and insight is gained. This testing-and-adjusting phase can last a long time, sometimes indefinitely, and that's normal.

Action is when a person is actively making changes in their behaviors, routines, habits, communication. This is where change becomes visible. It is also where it feels very effortful.

In this stage, people might experiment with trying something new or doing something differently. It's very common in this stage to experience both wins and setbacks, to feel both proud and discouraged, and to revise and create revisions when things don't go out as expected. I support action by helping the client to implement their plan. I asked them how they can use their skills, how they can use their strengths, and I facilitate problem-solving. I support finding alternative actions, if setbacks occur.

After action comes **maintenance**. In this stage, a person has already made meaningful changes and is working to maintain them over time. The challenge here is staying engaged, protecting progress, and continuing to choose behaviors that support and reinforce the change. This stage is not passive. It is an active stage to protect what has been created or built.

It can be helpful to practice new habits consistently, become aware of triggers earlier, continue to use supports, uphold established boundaries, and rely on helpful coping strategies. I strongly encourage clients to celebrate incremental progress and accomplishments here, while also acknowledging the vulnerability to setbacks, especially early in maintenance.

My role here is to help support consistency, resilience, and flexibility. The key message is that sustaining change requires attention, not perfection. This can be achieved with reinforcement of progress and growth, by helping to identify triggers and warning signs, normalizing any setbacks without treating them as failure, strengthening what is working and revising what is necessary, and helping someone to begin to see change as part of their new identity.

There is also another stage, often labeled **relapse**, which we'll spend time dissecting, exploring and reframing in an upcoming chapter. This deserves a deeper dive, because the way we understand and talk about this stage plays a critical role in whether people stay engaged with change or abandon it altogether.

Stages of Change: Quick Reference

- **Denial:** I don't really see the problem.
- **Precontemplation:** Something feels off, but I'm not sure what.
- **Contemplation:** I can see the problem, but I feel ambivalent.
- **Preparation:** I've decided something needs to change and I'm thinking about how.
- **Action:** I'm actively doing something differently.
- **Maintenance:** I'm working to keep the change going.
- **Relapse / Return to Old Patterns:** Something pulled me back, and I need to understand what happened.

Stage Check: Where Are You Right Now?

Rather than asking, *Am I ready?* try asking: *Where am I in the process?* See which of the following feels the most familiar, or sounds like you right now.

Denial (There isn't really a problem.)

"I don't think it's that big of a deal."

"Everyone's overreacting."

"I'm fine."

"This is just how I am."

You may not fully recognize that something needs to change. Even if there are consequences, they may feel unrelated, exaggerated, or unclear.

Precontemplation (Something feels off, but I'm not sure what.)

"Something isn't working… I just don't know what."

"I feel stuck, but I can't explain why."

"I keep ending up in the same place."

"I know something needs to change."

You're beginning to sense that something isn't working, but clarity is still forming.

Contemplation *(Why should I change?)*

"Part of me wants to… but part of me doesn't."

"I know something isn't working… I just don't know what to do."

"I'm not ready yet."

You're aware of the problem, but feeling ambivalent.

Preparation *(How will I change?)*

"I can't keep doing this."

"I need to figure this out."

"What if I tried ______?"

You've decided to make a change, and you're starting to make a plan.

Action *(I'm doing it.)*

"This is harder than I expected."

"I messed up."

"I'm trying, but it's not perfect."

You're actively making changes, albeit imperfectly.

Maintenance (I'm keeping it going.)

"This is working… I just need to stay consistent."

"I don't want to fall back into old patterns."

"I'm doing better, but I still have to be intentional."

You've made changes and are working to sustain them over time.

Gaining Clarity

One of the most common places people get stuck is believing they are "ready" while still being unclear about what actually needs to change. Many people feel motivated, fed up, or exhausted by the status quo, and yet nothing shifts. Often, this isn't a motivation problem, because it's **a clarity problem.** You can't solve the right problem if you haven't identified it yet.

For example, imagine someone who feels frustrated at work because they've been passed over for a promotion multiple times. They believe the issue is a lack of concrete skills, so they enroll in continuing education courses and certifications. On the surface, they look highly motivated and proactive. But the real issue may be something else entirely, such as chronic time management difficulties.

This pattern doesn't just show up at work. Friends feel frustrated when this person arrives late to events. Their partner feels hurt when promised timelines aren't honored. Until the belief about *what the problem actually is* gets revised, change can't fully take hold, regardless of how much effort is applied elsewhere. Once the real issue is acknowledged, meaningful change can ripple across many areas of life.

Another common example is smoking or vaping. Many people believe the problem is the cigarette or vape itself. But for some, smoking is actually a symptom; a way of coping with anxiety in social situations, regulating emotion, or managing discomfort. When the behavior is treated without understanding the underlying function it serves, change often doesn't last. When the real issue is addressed, the behavior may no longer be needed.

Another example shows up often around achievement, comparison, and self-worth.

Consider someone who is deeply self-critical and constantly measuring himself against others. He believes he hasn't "made it" because other people are more successful, earn more money, or appear stronger, financially and physically. He holds the belief that power, status, and physical strength are the true measures of worth. From the outside, it looks like a motivation problem. He pushes himself harder at work. He trains more intensely at the gym. He sets higher and higher standards for himself, yet never feels satisfied. No matter how much he does, it never feels like enough.

But the real issue isn't effort.

As the work unfolds, it becomes clear that these beliefs didn't come out of nowhere. Growing up with emotional neglect and physical abuse taught him something very specific: being powerful meant being protected. Strength, both physical and financial, became a way to stay safe in a world that once felt unpredictable and dangerous.

In adulthood, the strategy no longer fit the environment, but the belief remained. Competing, striving, and comparing weren't about ambition; they continued to be about survival.

Once he was able to name and acknowledge the abuse and neglect he experienced, something shifted. He no longer needed to prove his worth through dominance or achievement. The relentless comparison softened. He began to redefine success not as being the strongest or the wealthiest, but as being someone who was kind, reliable, and emotionally present for the people he chose to keep close. Originally, he believed the problem was that he wasn't doing enough, professionally or physically. In reality, the problem was that he was still trying to protect himself from a danger that no longer existed. Until the real issue was understood, no amount of effort could create lasting relief.

This is why people can feel "ready" and still remain stuck. They may be working hard, just not on the right thing yet.

When someone is working on the wrong problem, it can bring up feelings and emotions that can be cues this is occurring. Frustration, exasperation, confusion, aggravation, feeling like you're "spinning my wheels" or that "nothing is changing" can be cues that there is a mismatch between problem and solution. It feels heavy, like doing a lot of work without a payoff. Or like standing in quicksand.

Why People Stay Stuck

Change tends to occur when **the discomfort of staying the same becomes greater than the discomfort of changing**. But that balance is different for everyone. Sometimes what keeps people stuck isn't laziness or lack of willpower, it's that the current situation, while uncomfortable, is familiar. Predictability can feel safer than uncertainty, even when it's painful. In some cases, the struggle itself has become part of a person's identity, and letting go of it can feel destabilizing.

Another reason people remain stuck is waiting for the *perfect* moment, the perfect plan, the perfect clarity, or the perfect amount of confidence. But waiting for perfection often becomes a sophisticated form of avoidance. Change rarely begins when everything feels settled and certain. It begins when someone is willing to act with incomplete information, mixed emotions, and some degree of discomfort.

This is also where understanding **what is within your control, and what is not, becomes essential**. You can control your behavior, your boundaries, your effort, and your willingness to look honestly at patterns. You cannot control outcomes, other people's responses, timing, or whether change feels comfortable. Understanding what is within your control, and what is not, becomes essential.

You can control:

- your behavior
- your effort
- your response
- your boundaries
- your willingness to look honestly at patterns

You cannot control:

- outcomes
- other people
- timing
- whether change feels comfortable - to you or to others

Take a moment to think about, or perhaps take a few notes on, other items you could put into the two categories above.

In my work with clients, I've seen change happen in ways that are completely unpredictable. Sometimes it's a single thought, a final piece of information, or a moment of self-honesty that tips the decisional balance. Other times, change unfolds unexpectedly, after long periods of resistance or ambivalence. Understanding all of the ways change actually happens makes it far more realistic, achievable, and sustainable.

Rather than asking, *"Am I ready?"* A more useful question is: **What would need to shift for change to become possible right now?** What is truly within my control? And what might I still be misunderstanding about the problem itself?

What's Actually Getting in the Way

Before moving into action, it's essential to identify what might interfere with change. Barriers are not a sign that you aren't ready or capable; they are information. When barriers remain unnamed, people often interpret difficulty as personal failure. When barriers are identified clearly, change becomes more realistic and far more sustainable.

Barriers generally fall into two categories: **internal** and **external**.

Internal barriers are often rooted in beliefs, assumptions, or habitual ways of thinking.

These can include deeply held ideas about yourself or the world, such as *"I'm not capable," "I always mess things up," "It won't matter if I try,"* or *"This is just how I am."* Internal barriers also show up as subtle forms of self-protection: perfectionism, overthinking, avoidance, procrastination, or convincing yourself that now isn't the right time. These patterns developed for a reason, often to protect you from disappointment, failure, or rejection. The issue isn't that they exist, it's that they can keep you from starting at all.

External barriers, on the other hand, are often grounded in reality.

Work demands. Time limitations. Financial pressure. Health concerns. Caregiving responsibilities. Emotional labor. These are not excuses. These are real constraints that shape what is possible in your life right now. Ignoring external barriers doesn't make you more disciplined; it sets you up to fail by designing change that doesn't fit your actual circumstances. Sometimes external barriers aren't dramatic, they're constant and practical demands. Household chores. Pickups and drop-offs. Making dinner every night, including the planning, preparation, and cleanup. Managing schedules, responsibilities, and other people's needs. These demands quietly consume time, energy, and mental space, making reprioritization feel impossible even when motivation is present. When these realities go unacknowledged, people often blame themselves for "not following through," when the real issue is capacity, not commitment.

It's also crucial for me to say this clearly: **for anyone who has ever felt stuck, experienced depression or low mood, lived with chronic anxiety, ADHD, or other mental health challenges, doing something is not always simple.** At times, it can feel genuinely impossible. This isn't a lack of desire or effort. It's what happens when energy, focus, motivation, and emotional regulation are compromised. Naming this is essential, because shame thrives in silence and misunderstanding.

Identifying barriers is not about removing every obstacle before you move forward. It's about working with reality instead of against it. When you can clearly name what's in your way, both internally and externally, you stop fighting invisible forces. You can begin to design a change that accounts for your real life, your real limits, and your real responsibilities.

This awareness sets the stage for meaningful action. Not forced action, not performative change, but movement that has a chance to last.

Not All Inaction is Avoidance

Sometimes when something isn't getting done, the immediate conclusion is: "I'm avoiding it." And sometimes that's true, but not always. Not all inaction is avoidance. Sometimes what looks like avoidance is actually about capacity, burnout, or fear. Understanding the difference is helpful, because each one needs a different kind of response.

Avoidance is when you are able to do something, but you're intentionally or unconsciously steering away from it, usually because it feels uncomfortable. You might distract yourself, procrastinate, or convince yourself you'll "do it later." Avoidance is often driven by short-term relief. You don't do the thing, and you feel better temporarily, but the discomfort usually comes back, often stronger. The key feature of avoidance is: you *could* do it, but you're not.

Capacity, which we discussed earlier in *Part I: Assess,* asks a different question: *Do I actually have what I need right now to do this?* This includes time, energy, emotional bandwidth, and resources. When capacity is low, there may simply not be enough available to follow through. Pushing through low capacity often leads to more stress or shutdown. The key question becomes: Do I have the ability to do this right now, as I am?

Burnout is what happens when capacity has been exceeded for too long without adequate recovery. It often shows up as exhaustion, detachment, reduced motivation, and a sense that even simple tasks feel overwhelming. In burnout, it's not that you don't care—it's that your system is depleted. What used to feel manageable now feels heavy. The response burnout needs is not more pressure. It's rest, restoration, and recalibration.

Fear can look like avoidance, but it has a slightly different flavor. Fear is about perceived risk, of failure, rejection, judgment, or the unknown. You may want to take action, but something inside feels unsafe. This can show up as hesitation, overthinking, perfectionism, or waiting until you feel "ready." The key feature of fear is: part of you wants to move forward, and part of you is trying to protect you.

It helps to ask yourself what is actually happening here. ***Is this avoidance, or is it something else entirely?*** When you understand the difference, you can respond more effectively. Avoidance may call for gentle accountability. Low capacity may require adjustment. Burnout requires rest. Fear often needs support, safety, and smaller steps forward. And sometimes, it's a combination of more than one thing.

"I'm Not Ready" vs. "I'll Start Monday"

Finally, "I'm not ready" is often real. It may reflect lack of clarity, lack of support, lack of resources, or a real mismatch between what you're asking of yourself and what your current life can hold.

When someone says, *"I'm not ready,"* it can mean that something still needs attention before action makes sense. There may be unanswered questions, emotional resistance, competing demands, or a lack of capacity that would make change unsustainable right now. In these moments, "not ready" can provide a lot of information. It's your system signaling that something needs to be understood, adjusted, or supported before moving forward. When approached with honesty, "I'm not ready" can actually be a responsible and self-aware starting point.

On the other hand, *"I'll start Monday"* often reflects intention paired with hesitation. It's the part of you that wants to move forward, but is still negotiating the when and how. Sometimes it's about wanting a clean slate, a clear starting point, or a sense of control. Other times, it can be a subtle way of postponing discomfort while still feeling like you're doing something about it. The key difference is whether that time is being used intentionally—to prepare, plan, or build readiness—or whether it becomes an open-ended delay.

And honestly, I'm a huge fan of "I'll start Monday" energy. It means the intention is there. Maybe you're not ready and that's OK. Beating yourself up about not starting doesn't make any sense because it takes energy away from the action you need to move forward. So be gentle, be kind, and be compassionate with yourself.

Often, I tell people that it can take up to seven starts before habit sticks, and that 75% of all statistics are made up. That's a joke, but one that provides normalization that there can be starts and stops, procrastination, and multiple attempts made. You can start on Monday.

Before You Continue

Readiness is about understanding where you are in the process of change well enough to respond honestly and effectively. You explored change as something staged, fluid, and non-linear. You looked at the difference between wanting change and being prepared for it, and you considered how people can remain stuck when they misidentify the problem, work on the wrong target, or overlook the barriers standing in their way. You also began to distinguish between avoidance, low capacity, burnout, fear, and genuine unreadiness, because each of these experiences carries different information and calls for a different response.

That distinction is key.

When you understand what stage you are in, what is actually getting in the way, and what is within your control, action becomes more intentional and more sustainable. You begin to match your efforts to your reality. You approach yourself with more accuracy and less judgment. And you move forward in a way that is aligned, rather than forced.

This is what readiness offers: direction, clarity, and a starting point that fits.

Now that you've taken the time to understand your readiness, the next step is to begin moving. Not all at once, but intentionally. This is where you begin to activate.

Pause and Reflect

Take a moment to pause and reflect, without trying to fix or solve anything.

- Which stage of change do I feel most aligned with right now?
- What might I be misidentifying as the problem?
- When you struggle to follow through, what might be getting in the way that deserves understanding rather than criticism?

- What is actually getting in the way—avoidance, capacity, burnout, fear, or something else?
- What is one small step that fits where I am right now?

8

YOUR ACTIVATION

To FEEL BETTER, you need to take action. You need to do something, anything, to begin interrupting the patterns you're in and create change. Even the smallest something counts.

If you've ever experienced depression, anxiety, or ADHD, you may know firsthand how difficult it can be to activate when you feel overwhelmed, stuck, or paralyzed. When everything feels heavy, even simple tasks can feel out of reach.

And this isn't only true for people who are struggling. Even those who are functioning well, who feel generally stable or successful, can find themselves stuck when it comes to making a change, starting something new, or following through on what they already know would help.

Avoidance, while often protective in the short term, tends to reinforce the very patterns that keep you stuck. It creates a loop: the less you do, the harder it becomes to do anything at all. Fortunately, the opposite is also true. Action creates movement. Movement builds momentum.

This is where behavioral activation comes in. It is the shift from insight to concrete action. It is based on a powerful and often counterintuitive idea: motivation doesn't always come first. More often, it follows behavior.

If you are waiting to feel motivated, confident, or fully ready before you begin, you may be waiting longer than necessary. Change doesn't require perfect conditions. It requires a starting point. Small, achievable actions, ones that match your current capacity, can begin to shift how you feel, how you think, and what you do. Over time, those small actions build into something much larger.

Now that you've explored your readiness, this is where you begin to activate. Intentionally, and in a way that actually works.

Behavioral Activation: The Moment to Take Action Has Arrived

You have to do **something**.

You have to **do** something.

You **have** to do something.

You have to do something.

See what I did there? Please read it again.

Rarely am I this directive with clients. I'm typically collaborative, curious, and exploratory. But behavioral activation is one area where I am unapologetically clear: **if you want to feel better, or if you want something in your life to change, you have to do something.**

Not everything. Not the perfect thing. Just *something*.

Behavioral activation is based on a simple, often misunderstood truth: **behavior changes mood more reliably than mood changes behavior.** We tend to believe we need to feel motivated, confident, or ready *before* we act. In reality, motivation often shows up *after* action — not before it.

When someone is depressed, overwhelmed, or stuck, avoidance can take over. Less activity leads to lower mood, lower energy, and more avoidance. Functioning decreases. Pleasure disappears. Confidence erodes. This creates a kind of negative feedback loop: the less you do, the worse you feel, and the worse you feel, the less you do.

This is called **decompensation.**

The good news?

The reverse is also true.

Small actions, even painfully small ones, can start a **positive feedback loop**.

Action leads to a slight shift in mood or energy. That shift makes the next action a little more possible. Over time, momentum builds. Not because things suddenly feel easy, but because your nervous system and brain begin to register *movement* instead of stagnation.

Behavioral activation works because it bypasses overthinking and targets the system directly. Because when you're stuck, your brain is often waiting for a shift in motivation, clarity, or energy before taking action. But those states don't reliably come first. In many cases, they follow behavior, not the other way around.

This is where many people get stuck. They believe they need to feel confident, ready, or motivated before they begin.

When you take action, even a small one, several things begin to shift. Your mood may lift slightly. Your energy may change. You gain information. You interrupt patterns of avoidance. And perhaps most importantly, you begin to rebuild a sense of self-trust, the experience of *"I said I would do something, and I did."*

Each time you follow through, even imperfectly or reluctantly, you create evidence that you are capable of acting in your own best interest. Over time, that evidence accumulates. And that accumulation is what creates momentum.

Set the Bar *Very* Low (Lower Than You Think)

This is where we need to be very intentional.

One of the most common mistakes people make when trying to feel better is setting goals that are far too large for their current capacity. Lofty goals feel inspiring on good days and really crushing on tough ones.

When I work with clients, we're typically meeting weekly or biweekly, especially at first. So an activation plan is usually built for one week or two, and nothing longer than that. Most of the time, I'll help someone choose one, two, or three very small behavioral activation goals. The number depends on where we're starting.

For someone who hasn't been functioning well, the goal may simply be to begin again. That might mean something enjoyable, something grounding, or something that gently reconnects them with their body or environment.

Examples might include:

- open the blinds each morning
- make the bed more days than not this week
- step outside for five minutes
- text one person
- move into a different room instead of staying in bed
- wash your hands, brush your teeth, or take a shower

For someone who feels overwhelmed, activation may need to focus on reducing pressure rather than increasing output. One helpful task might be making a morning list with:

- one essential task
- two or three bonus tasks

- And then practicing tolerating an unfinished list without treating it like failure.

For someone who is shut down, I might encourage a small act of connection, movement, or body-based care. For someone who is overthinking everything, I usually want action over analysis: choose one thing you typically overthink, and do it before your brain turns it into a committee meeting.

If you're already functioning pretty well overall, activation may look different. At that stage, the question is often less "How do I get myself to do something?" and more "Is what I'm doing aligned with what I value most?"

For you, activation may look like:

- doing less, but more intentionally
- saying no to what no longer fits
- protecting time for rest, creativity, or connection
- noticing where you're overextending out of habit or identity
- adjusting direction slightly, instead of overhauling your life

When you're functioning well, the signals are often less obvious because you're compensating or have learned how to manage. It may not look like burnout or shutdown. It may look like going through the motions. Feeling disconnected. Losing excitement. Doing a lot, but not necessarily moving in the right direction.

As you begin to think about your own behavioral *activation* you might ask:

What is the smallest, most achievable action I could take today that moves me forward?

This question is not asking for the most impressive action, the most productive action, or the version you think you "should" be able to do. It is asking you to identify the most *doable* action that is *achievable*. You need to be able to clear the bar you set for yourself.

Sometimes it helps to see what "setting the bar low" actually looks like in real life:

- instead of clean the whole kitchen → empty the sink of dishes
- instead of go to the gym → put on sneakers and take a ten minute walk
- instead of text everyone back → reply to one person
- instead of organize the whole room → clear one surface
- instead of meditate for twenty minutes → deep breathing for five minutes
- instead of take care of yourself perfectly today → do one thing that demonstrates self-care

And yes, I often get a little chuckle from clients when we talk about this, because more often than not, they suggest something that is still way too ambitious. Nine times out of ten (and remember, 75% of statistics are made up, there's that joke again) I end up saying, "That's too high. Aim lower."

Perfectionists and high achievers usually look at me with giant, startled eyes, because it may be the first time anyone has told them to aim low on purpose. But I mean it. We want the goal low enough that success is likely, because success is what snowballs. Others think that they need to please me, which I address directly. This is fairly common: the feeling that they need to please the therapist, so they say something they think I want to hear.

A Quick Side Note

It's not uncommon for clients to find themselves trying to please their therapist, even if they are not fully aware they're doing it. This can look like agreeing with feedback, overstating progress, downplaying struggles, or avoiding topics that feel uncomfortable or disappointing.

It makes sense. Many people are used to being evaluated. Many have learned that approval leads to safety, connection, or acceptance. In therapy, though, that dynamic can get in the way, because growth depends on honesty, not performance.

A good therapist should notice this possibility and name it directly when it appears, helping to create a space where the client doesn't feel graded, judged, or expected to get it "right." And for clients, it can be helpful to remember: there is nothing to prove here. Saying "I didn't do the thing" or "This didn't work for me" is often more useful than reporting a polished success.

I once worked with a client who was severely depressed. She had recently started medication and was experiencing just enough relief to consider doing *something*. We agreed to create a list of three tiny, concrete, achievable tasks — not to "fix" her depression, but to reintroduce movement into her life. To *reactivate* her.

Her list looked like this:

- Pick up her tablet, hold it above her head, and say out loud: *"I did it."*
- Take out the bathroom trash once.
- Choose a single page in a mindfulness coloring book and color it.

That was it.

At that point, she hadn't engaged in activities she enjoyed, like reading, in months. Household tasks felt overwhelming. Her functioning was impaired. These actions may sound insignificant, but they weren't. Some of you will understand how monumental brushing your teeth or taking a shower can be! Each one of the items on this client's list represented engagement instead of avoidance, agency instead of helplessness, and proof that movement was possible.

One reason enjoyable activity can be so impactful, especially when someone is depressed or shut down, is that depression often reduces contact with pleasure, reward, and reinforcement. Behavioral activation works in part by helping people reconnect with activities that provide even small experiences of interest, enjoyment, accomplishment, or meaning. Over time, increasing contact with rewarding experiences can help shift mood and reduce the withdrawal-and-avoidance loop that depression tends to reinforce.

This does not mean every pleasant activity creates an instant emotional turnaround. Rather, re-engaging with something enjoyable or meaningful gives your brain and nervous system new information: movement is possible, pleasure is possible, connection is possible, and that life can contain more than stress, exhaustion, and getting through the day. Even modest increases in rewarding activity are part of how behavioral activation helps improve depressive symptoms over time.

There is a meaningful difference between a small, achievable action and a lofty goal.

"Go for a forty-five-minute workout" and "put on sneakers and step outside for one minute" are not the same task, neurologically or emotionally.

Notice that the very first task on the list above was simply to pick up the tablet, hold it up, and say out loud, *"I did it."* This client was an avid reader. Reading had once been a pastime she enjoyed and found deeply rewarding. But in that moment, actually reading felt like too much.

Starting small, by just picking the tablet back up, created success. And that success created momentum. Over time, it could lead to curiosity about what was on the device, perhaps scrolling through titles, then selecting something to look at, and eventually reading a few words or a paragraph. Not because she forced herself to, but because re-engagement became possible again.

Behavioral activation is about **starting where you are and trying to create small successes.**

You are not lazy for struggling to act. You are likely depleted, overwhelmed, or caught in an avoidance loop that once served a protective purpose. In those moments, action is not a reward for feeling better; **action is the intervention.**

Waiting for Motivation

When someone tells me they're waiting to feel motivated, I usually want to know more. What exactly do they mean by motivated? What does that feel like to them? Have they felt it before? What did it look like then? Because sometimes "motivation" really means certainty. Sometimes it means confidence. Sometimes it means the absence of discomfort. And if that is the standard, a person may wait a very long time before beginning.

One of my favorite mantras for this work came from a client: **better, not perfect.** I love that. It reminds us that improvement counts. Effort counts. Perfection is not the goal.

When clients begin behavioral activation, they are often focused on outcomes. Did I do it perfectly? Did it fix the problem? Do I feel completely better? And when the answer is no, the quick conclusion is often: this isn't working!

So I ask them to shift their focus to the evidence. There are real benefits to keeping track of small wins. When the focus shifts to the evidence, something changes. Instead of asking, "Did this fix everything?" we begin asking: Did you show up at all? Did you move even a little? Did your mood shift by even 5%? Did you tolerate something you used to avoid?

Those are very different questions. They are not "all-or-nothing" questions—and remember, all-or-nothing thinking is a common cognitive distortion!

Real change happens when they stop asking, "Did this fix it? Did it fix everything?" and start asking, "Did this help, even a little?" Because a little is repeatable. Little efforts can be repeated over and over, and that's how change is created.

Change is made through small wins that add up over time.

A Simple Activation Log

Sometimes a simple activation log can be very helpful when you're trying to track behavioral change. It can be hard to see overall progress when you're in the middle of it, and it's easy to miss the small successes along the way.

When I introduce this to clients, I like to keep it straightforward: this is not a full journal. You're not writing paragraphs. You're not analyzing your childhood. You're collecting a few pieces of information.

You can do this on your phone, on another device, or the old-school way with pen and paper. You might decide to use an app. There are plenty of them. Some make tracking easy, some try to gamify the experience, and some probably act like an overenthusiastic accountability coach. None of them, to my knowledge, shock you like an electric fence if you miss a task. That's a joke. And fortunately, the research we do have tends to favor reinforcement over punishment when it comes to sustaining behavior change.

After you complete a small task, something simple, intentional, and aligned with what you're working on, briefly note the following:

- What did I do?
- How did I feel before I did it?
- Was there resistance beforehand? (yes/no or low/medium/high)
- Did I follow through?
- How did I feel after?
- Did it help at all — even 1%?

That's it. This should take less than a minute.

The purpose of this log is to gather evidence. It isn't reflection for the sake of reflection. It's data collection. It helps you track behavior, notice patterns, and create a record that your mood and memory may not reliably provide. Because when you feel unmotivated, your brain can get dramatic:

"Nothing helps." "I never follow through." "What's the point?"

But when you actually track what is happening, something different may emerge. You may begin to notice that you often feel worse before you start but then feel better afterwards, or that resistance shows up, but you can still act. Maybe your mood shifts, even slightly, after doing the thing. Those small actions really do have an impact.

This kind of tracking helps interrupt the narrative that "nothing works."

And look, I get it. Who wants another item added to an already never-ending list of things to do? I certainly don't. So if you immediately feel oppositional to the idea of tracking, would you be willing to try it for just a week or two? Please remember that I'm not asking you to write pages. You're not doing a deep emotional dive. You're just jotting down a few observations so your brain stops guessing about whether what you're doing is helping.

It turns: "I never do anything" into "I did three small things this week, even though I didn't feel like it."

It turns: "Nothing helps" into "It helps a little… and a little counts."

Hierarchy of Change: Starting Small on Purpose

Creating a hierarchy of change is a way of approaching growth with intention, safety, and respect for your nervous system. Instead of jumping straight into the most difficult or uncomfortable version of a change, this approach starts with smaller, more manageable steps, ones that feel relatively low-stakes and non-threatening. These early steps build the foundation. They build familiarity, confidence, and a sense of control. Larger, more challenging changes are placed later in the process, to be approached only after your body and mind have had time to adapt.

I often talk with clients about this as **starting small on purpose**, because forcing yourself into a bigger change too quickly often backfires. When change feels overwhelming or unsafe, the nervous system does what it's designed to do: it resists.

This idea is closely related to exposure therapy, where people gradually and repeatedly engage with situations they fear or avoid in a structured way. Rather than overwhelming yourself or white-knuckling your way through discomfort, the goal is learning. Through repeated experience, the nervous system begins to understand, *I can tolerate this. I don't need to avoid it.* Each successful step reduces reactivity and increases capacity, making the next step feel more accessible.

A hierarchy of change works because it honors how trust, especially trust in yourself, actually develops: through repetition, predictability, and choice. Change becomes less about forcing yourself and more about building a cooperative relationship with your own system.

Here's an example. One client wanted to stop being a chronic people-pleaser. She knew this pattern was draining her, but she didn't feel ready to advocate for herself in big, high-stakes ways. Negotiating the price of a home improvement project felt completely out of reach. Too risky. Too uncomfortable. So we didn't start there.

Instead, we identified low-stakes opportunities to practice the same skill. She began by telling a restaurant server that her food was incorrect. She practiced sending a text to decline an invitation without over-explaining or apologizing. These moments felt uncomfortable, but they were manageable and they were safe. Each one was a small win. Each one became evidence: *I can do this. The discomfort passes. I survived.*

Over time, those wins stacked up. And once you have enough evidence that you can tolerate discomfort and advocate for yourself, the stakes can rise, gradually, intentionally, and on your terms. What once felt impossible begins to feel doable.

This is how confidence actually builds. Not through hype or positive thinking, but through lived experience. When you repeatedly show yourself that you are capable, your system begins to believe it. And from there, change becomes something you grow into one step at a time.

Top-Down and Bottom-Up Change

In mental health care, we often talk about change in terms of *where it begins*.

Some change starts **top-down**, through thinking and insight. Other change starts **bottom-up**, through action, the body, and the environment. Both are valid. Both are powerful. And most lasting change involves a combination of the two.

Top-down change begins with the mind. It focuses on noticing, examining, and revising thoughts, beliefs, and interpretations that shape emotional experience and behavior. This includes insight, cognitive restructuring, meaning-making, and narrative shifts, all of which engage the thinking brain to create new understanding. When the story you're telling yourself changes, the way you feel often changes with it.

This is why we began in the *Align* section by working with your thinking. Before asking you to act differently, we needed to understand what you were telling yourself about who you are, what's possible, and what things mean. Changing behavior without addressing these underlying narratives often leads to resistance, burnout, or self-blame.

Here's an example of top-down change. One client had very strong feelings about taking medication. She viewed medication as something "lazy people" used instead of making lifestyle changes. After feeling lousy for years with a variety of symptoms, and finding that nothing else was helping her manage perimenopause, she was faced with a decision: stay the same, or reconsider how she was thinking about treatment.

For her, the shift began cognitively. She worked on loosening the rigid belief that medication meant weakness. Once she allowed some flexibility in thinking, new possibilities opened:

- medication is a tool I can use to support my health
- medication is for healthy people too

- medication may help support the healthy lifestyle I've been struggling to maintain because my symptoms are untreated

That top-down shift created room for different action.

Bottom-up change starts somewhere else entirely. It begins with the body, behavior, and environment. It recognizes that nervous system states, routines, sleep, nutrition, movement, sensory input, and external conditions profoundly influence mood, motivation, and capacity. Bottom-up work can include behavioral activation, movement, sleep regulation, grounding strategies, sensory regulation, exposure work, nutrition, or changes in daily structure and environment.

Sometimes people don't feel better because they had a breakthrough. Sometimes they feel better because they finally slept consistently, started eating regularly, spent less time in survival mode, or changed a daily pattern that had been draining them.

Bottom-up work can also help create the stability needed for deeper cognitive and emotional work. When the nervous system feels less overwhelmed, people often have greater access to reflection, flexibility, emotional regulation, and problem-solving.

Insight can open the door. Action helps you walk through it.

Here's a bottom-up example. One client felt incredibly overwhelmed. She had a new job, was preparing for an out-of-state move, was finishing graduate school, and still had to do all the ordinary tasks of being an adult, including taxes. Any one of those would have been stressful. Together, they were crushing her. She wasn't confused about what was happening. Her thoughts were grounded, realistic, and valid. What she noticed most was the pressure in her body.

So rather than starting with her thoughts, we started with action. Historically, high-intensity exercise had been one of the best ways for her to release stress, think clearly, and sleep better. So she committed to five minutes of high-intensity movement. That was enough to shift something in her system.

That strategy makes sense physiologically, too. Movement can improve sleep, reduce stress, and support emotional regulation. It does not solve every problem, but it can change the state of the body enough to make coping easier.

Another client was grieving the loss of a parent and desperately needed space to breathe and grieve. As many of you know, grief does not politely fit into a neat schedule. The world expects you to keep going, get back to work, answer the texts, do the things, while internally, nothing feels normal.

This client knew that being outdoors brought the most peace. There were financial considerations, but camping was possible. Two nights was what worked. That environmental change did not erase the grief, but it gave her space to be with it differently. Sometimes the change begins by changing where you are.

Where Behavioral Activation Fits

By now, you've already experienced the top-down side of this process. This is where **behavioral activation** comes in.

Behavioral activation is a **bottom-up** approach. Instead of starting with thoughts, it starts with action and environment. It's about doing something differently: changing routines, modifying surroundings, creating structure, and taking small, intentional steps that support the life you're trying to build. When you change what you do and what surrounds you, your nervous system and emotional state often follow.

Arguably, the most effective change happens when both approaches are used together. You change how you think *and* you do something about it.

One client felt trapped in a friendship that left her drained and resentful. On the surface, it looked like a behavioral problem: she kept showing up, kept answering texts, and kept offering support even when she had nothing left to give. But the real work started cognitively. She began to examine the story she was telling herself about the friendship.

She noticed the distorted thinking that kept her stuck. She reminded herself how much effort she had consistently put in and how little she received in return. She challenged the belief that she was responsible for this person's happiness, or that being a "good friend" meant providing endless support at her own expense. Slowly, the narrative shifted: a friendship should also meet *her* needs. That cognitive restructuring didn't end the friendship overnight, but it changed how she related to it. And once her thinking changed, her behavior followed. Boundaries became possible because they finally made sense.

Another client worked within a deeply dysfunctional school system. She often felt anxious and depressed, personalizing systemic failures and interpreting them as evidence that she wasn't doing enough. Through the top-down work of cognitive restructuring, she zoomed out. She began to see the bigger picture. Many of the issues she faced were limitations of the system itself, not personal shortcomings. She reminded herself that she showed up for students and colleagues with integrity and effort, even when outcomes were constrained. That shift in thinking changed how she felt.

The bottom-up work involved boundaries. She stopped responding to work emails at all hours. She created clear rules around when she would check and reply, rather than being available 24/7. That environmental change reduced stress, protected her energy, and reinforced the cognitive shift she had already made.

Sometimes change happens top-down.

Sometimes it happens bottom-up.

The most sustainable change usually involves both.

Sometimes you change how you think first, and then your behavior follows. Sometimes you act first, and your thinking catches up. Both count.

This is why we didn't start with doing before understanding, because action without clarity often leads to burnout. And it's why we didn't stop with insight, because understanding without action keeps people stuck.

When thinking and doing work together, change stops feeling forced. It starts to feel aligned.

Breaking It Down, Backwards

Sometimes the hardest part of change isn't motivation. It's knowing where to begin.

Therapists often use approaches like task-centered or solution-focused work to help people break overwhelming goals into smaller, more manageable steps. I think of it as creating a roadmap. It's pragmatic, clarifying, and highly satisfying. There is something deeply regulating about turning a big, intimidating goal into a series of smaller, more manageable steps, especially when those steps can be checked off, crossed out, or visibly completed. Progress becomes observable, not theoretical. And lots of us feel the dopamine hit when the box gets checked or the item is crossed off.

Sometimes it feels challenging to work towards a goal. You know the desired outcome, but aren't exactly sure where to begin.

You know something needs to shift. You may even know *what* you want to be different. But when you look at the big picture, it feels vague, overwhelming, or impossibly far away. When that happens, the brain often does what brains do best under stress: it shuts things down. Avoidance kicks in, not because you don't care, but because the goal feels too abstract to grasp.

This is where working backward can be incredibly helpful.

Rather than starting at the beginning and trying to push your way toward a distant outcome, you start at the finish line. You identify the end result you want, the change, the relief, the life you're moving toward, and then you ask, *What would need to happen just before that? And before that?* Step by step, the vague becomes concrete.

Working backward also helps your nervous system. Instead of relying on willpower or motivation alone, this approach builds structure. It highlights where obstacles might exist, what resources you'll need, and where flexibility or support will make a difference. The brain likes predictability. It likes knowing what comes next. And it especially likes frequent moments of completion, small wins that build confidence and momentum over time.

This way of thinking about goals also allows you to zoom out without panicking. You can ask yourself questions like: Where do I want to be in five years? (No, this is not a job interview.) What would I need to do this year to move in that direction? What would that look like this month? This week? Today?

You can use this framework in nearly every area of life — work, relationships, family dynamics, spirituality, health, hobbies, or simply creating more space for enjoyment. The goal is to create direction.

One client I worked with knew she wanted to leave an unhealthy relationship. She had already done the hardest part: the emotional labor required to admit that the relationship wasn't working and that she wanted something different. That process had taken time, courage, and a lot of internal reckoning. But once she reached that clarity, the *logistics* felt paralyzing. Thinking about everything that would need to be done made the task feel insurmountable, which stalled any movement forward.

Instead of asking her to "figure it all out," we worked backward. Starting with the outcome of leaving the relationship, she identified what would need to be in place over the next year, then the next few months, then the coming weeks. Untangling finances. Rebuilding independence. Creating emotional support. Each step became smaller, clearer, and more manageable. Motivation didn't come from forcing herself to act. It came from finally having a logical plan.

Working backward doesn't necessarily make the overall change easier, but it can make it easier to know where to begin.

Before You Continue

You've been encouraged to choose something—something enjoyable, something that reduces pressure, something that improves efficiency, strengthens a boundary, supports connection or communication, protects your peace, creates space for rest, adjusts your direction, or helps you stop overextending. Maybe it's a small step toward a larger goal. Maybe it's simply doing something differently.

It all counts.

You've also seen how this work connects to what we've already explored. We addressed changing thoughts in earlier chapters, and returned to it here through a top-down and bottom-up approach. You've learned that sometimes change begins with how you think, and other times it begins with what you do. Most often, it's both.

You've been invited to track your efforts through a simple activation log as a way to gather evidence. Because when you record the small things, the follow-through, the effort, the 1% shifts, something begins to change: you begin to challenge the belief that "nothing works." You start to see that something is working, even if it's gradual. And gradual is how change happens.

I understand that it can be hard, or at times *feel* impossible, to begin. (And notice I said *feel*. Because as we've already discussed, feelings aren't facts.)

Waiting for the perfect moment or for complete readiness tends to keep you in the same place. It reinforces the very patterns you're trying to shift. Movement, even small movement, interrupts that cycle. So if you take one thing from this, let it be this: do something. Not everything. Not perfectly. Just something.

Aim low on purpose! Because success builds from there.

Pause and Reflect

Take a moment to pause and reflect, without trying to fix or solve anything yet.

- What is one small action I could take that feels low-pressure but meaningful?
- Where might I be setting the bar too high for my current capacity?
- What tends to happen when I wait to feel motivated before I begin?
- Which kind of activation might support me most right now: pleasure, responsibility, connection, body care, environmental change, or something else?
- Am I more in need of top-down change, bottom-up change, or a combination of both?
- What evidence of effort or follow-through might I be overlooking because it feels "too small" to count?
- If I focused on better, not perfect, what would my next step look like?

9

YOUR CHANGE

YOU'VE STARTED TO ACTIVATE. You've identified something—even something small—that you can do to begin creating change.

Change can be hard! It takes conscious effort, ongoing investment, and a lot of energy. Early change can feel especially challenging because what you're doing isn't automatic yet, because you're building something new. It requires attention, awareness, and mindfulness.

When you begin to change, not everyone around you is going to be thrilled about it. Some people may be outspoken in their discomfort. Others may be more subtle. Passive, resistant, or pulling you back toward what's familiar. Not necessarily because they want to harm you, but because what's familiar feels safe to them, and to the system you've been part of. But you are allowed to disrupt that system. Even when it's uncomfortable or creates tension around you.

Setbacks will happen, too. They are a completely normal part of the change process. What counts is how you understand them. When framed as failure, setbacks can shut you down. But when understood as a source of new information, as feedback, or as reminders of what no longer works, they become part of your progress. The language you use here shapes that process.

As you continue to activate, remember this: change is not a destination. It's not a box you check or a place you arrive. It's a process that continues to unfold over time. Hopefully you will celebrate your successes along the way, because noticing what *is* working matters just as much as identifying what isn't.

We are moving toward the final part of this work, and I want to leave you with something practical. You've done a deep and thorough exploration, clinically called a comprehensive assessment, followed by an intentional plan for change.

Now I want to give you a way to continue this process after you finish the book. A way to *reassess*, *realign*, and *reactivate*—again and again, as needed.

Why Change Feels So Hard at First (and Why That Makes Sense)

When clients tell me, *"Why does this feel so hard if I'm doing the right thing?"* my first response is usually a question:

How long have you been doing the thing you're trying to change?

Most people pause… and then say, *"My whole life."* Sometimes that means twenty years. Sometimes thirty. Sometimes longer. And that's usually the moment things click.

Of course, this feels hard. You are doing something brand new. This isn't routine yet. You haven't practiced it. You haven't lived it long enough for it to feel automatic. What you're being asked to do right now requires intention, mindfulness, and effort, and that takes energy.

I'll often ask clients to think about another time in their life when something felt awkward, overwhelming, or exhausting at first, and then, later, it became second nature. Starting a new job is a perfect example. Even if you're highly skilled, everything is unfamiliar when you first begin. You don't know the systems, the culture, or where anything lives. At first, you're thinking about *everything*. Then two months in… six months in… you're doing your job without even realizing how much effort it once required. Maybe you're even at the point where you could train someone else.

Change works the same way.

One of the biggest misunderstandings about change is the belief that effort should come with immediate payoff. *I do the thing → I feel better right away.* Or that because motivation was high at the beginning, the daily reality should feel easier.

Take the person who decides to start a new morning routine. They plan it. Visualize it. Decide exactly how it will look. They go to bed feeling motivated and optimistic. Then the alarm goes off. Snooze. Again. Again. Again. Again. And the change didn't happen as planned. This phase is awkward. It's tiring. It requires attention. It requires effort, sustained mindfulness, and intention.

Here's the neurological piece, **the science behind the struggle.**

Your brain communicates through neural pathways, routes that send signals between different parts of the brain and nervous system. You can think of them like roads or trails. Every time you think a thought, feel a feeling, or take an action, signals travel along one of these paths. The more a path is used, the faster and easier it becomes — just like a trail becomes clearer the more people walk on it.

When you're young, your brain creates an enormous number of these pathways as it learns how the world works. Over time, it keeps the ones that are used most and lets others fade. This makes the brain efficient, but it also means that familiar reactions, especially those tied to safety, coping, and identity, can become automatic.

These well-worn pathways aren't bad. They're your brain doing exactly what it's designed to do: rely on what's known.

Change happens when you start using a different path.

At first, that path feels slow, clumsy, and effortful. You have to think about it. You have to pause. You have to redirect. But every time you choose that new response, you strengthen the pathway just a little bit more. Over time, the old path loses dominance, and the new one becomes easier to access.

If you've ever learned anything hard, you already understand this.

Musicians, this example is for you. Learning a new piece of music can be maddening. You read it slowly. You stop and restart. You practice the same measure over and over. Some sections flow easily; others feel impossible. And sometimes it feels like your fingers simply refuse to do what your brain knows they should do. Then one day… it clicks. The whole piece flows — even the hard parts — and you think, *Yes. I did it.* That's your brain building new neural pathways.

Same with video games. You get stuck at the same level. The same boss. The same jump. Over and over. Until your muscles learn the timing, your brain anticipates what's coming, and suddenly you can play straight through without thinking.

Change works exactly like this.

People often get discouraged when old behaviors resurface, especially when they're exhausted, overwhelmed, anxious, hungry, or burned out. When energy is low, the brain defaults to what requires the least effort, and this is the familiar path. If you're a visual person, imagine walking through fresh snow. It's much easier to step into footprints that already exist than to forge a brand-new trail. Under stress, your brain does the same thing.

That doesn't mean you've undone your work. It means you're normal.

Change does not become automatic all at once. At first, it requires intention, attention, and repetition. You have to catch yourself. Pause. Make a different choice.

Imagine someone who automatically apologizes for everything. At first, they don't even notice they're doing it. Then they start catching it after the fact. Eventually, they catch it in the moment: "Wait, I don't actually need to apologize for taking up space or asking a question." At first, choosing a different response feels uncomfortable and unnatural. Over time, though, the pause becomes easier and the new response requires less effort.

It feels awkward and tiring because you are asking your brain and nervous system to operate outside of familiar patterns. But with repetition, the process becomes less effortful. The pauses get shorter. The redirection feels more natural.

Eventually, the new response stops feeling forced. Not because you willed yourself into permanent change, but because your brain practiced a different pathway often enough for it to become more familiar and accessible. The old pathways are still there, but over time they are less dominant.

This is why small, repeated actions are more effective than dramatic bursts of effort. The brain learns through consistency. Real change happens when new patterns are practiced long enough to become familiar enough to use automatically. Of course this feels hard at first. You are practicing a different way of operating, and new patterns require more attention, energy, and repetition before they begin to feel natural.

A Personal Example: Values in Practice

I'll give you a personal example.

One of my core values is humor. For a long time, I thought that meant being funny, having quick wit, levity, and making light of situations. Over time, I realized that wasn't quite it. Not every moment calls for a joke, and not every situation should be treated lightly. What I actually value is finding humanity and connection through humor, even in dark or painful moments.

Once I clarified that, my reactions began to shift.

I didn't need to perform humor or force it. I started aligning my responses with the deeper value underneath it. The result wasn't constant laughter; it was authenticity, and that refinement changed how I showed up. It was about connection. Comfort. Humanity. Bringing light without minimizing darkness.

That distinction is important. Years ago, I needed an MRI. I was dressed in the standard-issue gown and socks, sitting in a cold waiting room, when another woman sat down nearby. Her body language screamed terror. We sat in silence for a moment. Then I gestured to our outfits and said, "I really like your look." She smiled. Just a little. Nothing magical happened. But I lived my value in that moment: offering warmth, connection, and humanity where I could. That's alignment.

I want to pause here to explain why I'm sharing this. In therapy, self-disclosure is used intentionally and sparingly. Therapists are trained to be thoughtful about when to share personal information and when to withhold it, always asking whether a disclosure serves the client and the work being done. Therapy is never meant to become about the therapist's story, needs, or experiences. The focus must stay on the client.

When a therapist does share something personal, it is brief, relevant, and offered in service of clarity, normalization, or connection, not to seek validation or create reciprocity. Many personal details are intentionally held back, even when a therapist could easily relate, because restraint is part of ethical and effective care.

This example isn't shared so you understand *me* better. It's shared to illustrate how values clarification actually works in real life. Alignment isn't static. You don't get it "right" once and lock it in forever. Values deepen. Meanings evolve. Flexibility in thinking means being able to change how you think or feel as new information becomes available.

You Are Allowed to Disrupt the System

Finally, we need to talk about context, because no one changes in isolation.

When you begin to change, the people and systems around you are affected, whether they want to be or not. Family Systems Theory explains this well. At its core, this theory recognizes that people don't exist as independent units; we exist within systems. Families, partnerships, workplaces, friend groups, and communities all function as interconnected networks where each person's behavior influences the whole.

A helpful way to imagine this is as a set of gears. Each gear turns in relation to the others. When one cog changes direction or speed, the entire machine has to adjust. If the rest of the gears don't move with it, there's friction. Grinding. Resistance. Noise. When you change, you are that moving gear.

Systems are wired to maintain balance, which therapists call *homeostasis*. Even when a system is unhealthy, it often prefers familiar dysfunction over unfamiliar change. Predictability feels safer than uncertainty. So when one person begins to behave differently, the system may push back because it is trying to return to what it knows.

Another way to think about this is gravity.

Old roles, expectations, and patterns exert a pull. When you try to move in a new direction, it can feel like something is tugging you back down through comments, guilt, pressure, disappointment, subtle disapproval. That pull doesn't mean you're weak. It means gravity exists.

Or imagine elastic bands.

For a long time, you and the people around you have been connected by invisible bands in the form of shared habits, roles, and expectations. When you start to move, the band stretches. At first, there's tension. If the system doesn't adapt, the band may snap back, pulling you toward your old position. This is often when people hear things like:

- "You've changed."
- "You used to be more fun."
- "Why are you making this such a big deal?"
- "Can't you just be like you were before?"

These reactions aren't always intentional or malicious. Often, they're driven by anxiety. When one person changes, others may feel pressure to change too or fear being left behind. The system becomes destabilized and seeks resolution.

There will be people who don't like what you're doing. Not necessarily because they want to harm you, but because they like you the way you are. You are familiar. Your patterns are familiar. And familiarity feels safe. When you change, others may feel unsettled and that discomfort can show up as resistance.

In close relationships, this often appears as a push–pull dynamic. When one person begins to pull away from old patterns, others may push harder to restore the previous balance. This is especially common when two people have been functioning in unhealthy but familiar ways and one starts moving toward something healthier. The other person may feel threatened, exposed, or pressured to examine their own behavior. They may also fear losing the relationship altogether.

Sometimes the system adapts.

Sometimes it resists.

Often, both happen at once.

Because of this, people frequently feel guilty or selfish for changing.

One client I worked with had a long-standing, difficult relationship with his father. Over time, he came to see that his father's emotional immaturity, gaslighting, and controlling behavior were not things he wanted close in his life anymore. He didn't want to cut his father off entirely, but he did want more distance — an arm's-length relationship instead of full access. Implementing those boundaries was deeply uncomfortable, especially at first. His father reacted strongly, and my client felt an immediate surge of guilt. Old "shoulds" appeared quickly: *I should want to be closer. I should call more. I should try harder.* Yet every time he returned to the familiar pattern, he left feeling agitated, frustrated, and unheard.

The work wasn't just about setting boundaries; it was about tolerating the discomfort that followed. He also carried a belief that others would see him as a bad person for not being close to his father. In one session, I asked him, "What if there were ten thousand times more people who would respect you for your ability to set and uphold boundaries?" He paused. He had never considered that perspective. And when he reflected honestly, he realized that the people who knew him best would understand his reasons completely.

Because of these dynamics, it's common to feel guilty or selfish for changing. When systems push back, many people assume they've done something wrong. But discomfort is not a reliable indicator of harm. Often, it is simply the cost of disrupting patterns that were never designed to support growth. When you move differently, friction is inevitable because the system is adjusting to a new pattern.

This is why sustainable change requires awareness of context, not just personal effort. Sometimes support shows up as encouragement and curiosity. Other times, it shows up as resistance that must be tolerated rather than fixed. In those moments, the work is not to convince others or smooth over discomfort, but to stay anchored in what you know to be true. That may mean redefining boundaries, limiting access to your inner world, or allowing relationships to evolve in ways that feel unfamiliar but necessary.

You are allowed to disrupt systems that depend on you staying the same. You are allowed to move toward what is healthier, even when others struggle to understand it. Other people's discomfort does not mean your change is wrong. Change does not require universal approval; it requires enough internal alignment to remain steady when others are unsettled. As relationships and systems adjust (or fail to adjust) the task is to stay grounded in what you know to be true, rather than pulled back by guilt or fear. You are allowed to let discomfort exist without treating it as a signal to stop. Growth rarely happens without impact.

Rethinking Setbacks: Language Shapes the Experience

When someone tells me they've had a setback, the first thing I pay attention to is *how they're talking about it*. Language matters here.

If a moment is framed as a *setback*, a *backslide*, a *failure*, or *starting over*, it automatically carries a negative charge. Those words tend to evoke disappointment, shame, frustration, and self-criticism. And once those feelings take hold, they often drive behaviors aimed at relief rather than growth — avoidance, giving up, or returning to familiar patterns.

But when the same moment is framed differently, as information, a reminder, a signal, or a learning opportunity, the emotional experience shifts. The person feels less defeated and more capable of re-engaging. This is classic cognitive-behavioral territory: a thought shapes a feeling, which then influences behavior. When someone returns to an old behavior or pattern they were trying to change, it doesn't mean they've erased their progress. More often, it means they've encountered a reminder of what they no longer want, a pattern they no longer need, or a strategy that no longer works for who they're becoming.

One of the most damaging assumptions people make is that a setback means they're "back at the beginning." They're not. Too much has happened since then: insight, effort, awareness, attempts, learning. None of that disappears because of one detour.

This is where understanding the *stages of change* becomes grounding. Change isn't linear. People move through denial, precontemplation, contemplation, preparation, action, and maintenance and often revisit earlier stages along the way. Moving back and forth is a normal part of the process. People learn, adjust, revisit old patterns, and try again.

There is also a stage often labeled *relapse*. Clinically, relapse simply refers to returning to an unwanted behavior. I've never loved that word. It sounds final and damning, as if progress has been erased. I prefer *hiccup*, *speed bump*, or *reminder*. These words acknowledge what happened without defining the person by it.

What This Looks Like in Real Life

One client decided to stop playing poker after recognizing that it had become compulsive. He enjoyed the dopamine hits, but when he lost, the financial consequences directly undermined his long-term goals. The behavior no longer aligned with the life he wanted.

He maintained abstinence for weeks, then months. One weekend, he gave in to the urge and lost a significant amount of money. On paper, it looked like he was back at the beginning — his savings account was back at zero.

But *he* wasn't.

That moment didn't erase the insight he had gained or the clarity about why poker no longer worked for him. Instead of interpreting the loss as failure, he was able to see it as confirmation, a reminder that this behavior no longer fit his values or goals. The money was gone, but the learning remained.

Another client wanted to change her relationship with alcohol. She recognized that heavy drinking wasn't good for her health and didn't align with her desire to focus on strength training, nutrition, and physical well-being. Rather than stopping entirely, she chose a harm reduction approach, which is something I strongly support. For many people, reducing harm feels more achievable, and success often builds momentum.

She made meaningful changes and felt better overall. Then she attended a friend's birthday celebration and drank more than she intended. Physically, she felt awful the next day — and yes, *hanxiety* is very real. But emotionally, something was different.

She didn't spiral into shame.

Instead, she felt reminded. Reminded of why she no longer wanted to live this way. In the past, that discomfort would have triggered more drinking to cope with the feelings. This time, reframing the experience as a reminder, rather than a failure, allowed her to move forward without undoing her progress.

Why the Frame Matters

Anyone who has ever worked with me knows I care deeply about language. We often slow down and examine the words being used, because the wrong word can reinforce shame, while the right one can preserve momentum.

Calling something a *failure* tends to shut people down. Calling it a *reminder* keeps the door open.

A setback doesn't mean you start over.

It means you start *from where you are*, with more information than you had before.

Change Is Not a Destination

Some people think of change as something you work toward, achieve, and then check off the list. And sometimes that *is* true: there are clear-cut changes with a beginning, middle, and end. But most meaningful change doesn't work that way. Change is rarely a destination. It's a practice.

People often imagine change as an action with a start and a finish, like running a 5K or a marathon. There's a starting line, some effort in the middle, maybe a cramp if you didn't stretch (no judgment), recovery afterward, and then it's done. It's an achievement.

But even in that example, something deeper is happening. Were you always a runner? Or did you have to align yourself with the values, habits, and identity of someone who trains? What qualities did you embody just to make it to the *starting line*, let alone the finish? Discipline. Commitment. Flexibility. Tolerance for discomfort. Those qualities don't disappear when the race is over!

As change unfolds, it's both helpful and necessary to revisit it. To review what's working and to notice what needs more support or adjustment. These observations provide information that helps shape what comes next.

In my work, whenever a client decides to take something from therapy into the real-life space between sessions, whether it's something to think about, something to try, or a specific assignment, I always say the same thing to them: not doing "the thing" can give us just as much information, and sometimes even more, than completing it. That's why I genuinely want clients to come back and tell me if something didn't happen. Avoidance, resistance, forgetting, or deciding it didn't fit all tell us something meaningful about what might be getting in the way.

Equally important, noticing what *is* working creates space for acknowledgment and celebration. Maintenance takes effort. Consistency takes work. Preventing setbacks, or responding to them in a healthy way, takes energy. Those wins are not accidental, and they deserve recognition. Paying attention to what works helps reinforce change and clarifies what is worth continuing.

One of the most common moments people mistake for failure is re-engaging in a behavior they had previously worked to change.

Here's an example.....

One client became consumed after a sudden breakup. She found herself engaging in behaviors she didn't recognize or like: driving by her ex's house, compulsively checking social media, calling her ex's workplace to see if she was on shift. Even she described these behaviors as "borderline creepy" and desperately wanted them to stop.

Context is essential here.

Her childhood included neglect. She had an anxious attachment style. She'd experienced rejection related to her sexuality. The breakup blindsided her. These behaviors didn't come from nowhere; they were attempts to manage unbearable anxiety and loss.

She did real work. She learned healthier ways to cope. She made progress. And then, one day, she called her ex's workplace again.

She *could* have labeled that moment as a failure. But what would that have accomplished? Shame? Discouragement? Withdrawal? Instead, we reframed it as information. This wasn't a collapse. It was a signal that additional support and coping strategies were still needed when anxiety spiked beyond what she could tolerate.

Not failure. Feedback.

Reassess → Realign → Reactivate

When change gets messy, and it will, this is the process I come back to again and again:

Reassess → Realign → Reactivate

Let's break it down.

Reassess: What's Actually Going On?

When I ask clients to reassess, I'm asking them to approach this with genuine curiosity rather than criticism. You've already done a lot of self-exploration, and once you know the questions to ask yourself, and what to look for, reassessment becomes easier. You are looking for new information.

Reassessment means taking a step back and looking honestly at what's happening right now, not what *should* be happening.

- Mood.
- Energy.
- Sleep.
- Nutrition.
- Relationships.
- Physical Health.
- Medication.
- Expectations.
- Cognitive or emotional load.
- Alignment with values.

Some of the first questions I ask are simple but powerful:

Has anything obvious happened?

Sometimes clients overlook major stressors because they've been "handling it." I once reviewed six weeks with someone that included a job change, a move, an illness, and multiple social obligations. When I said, "No wonder you're exhausted," it genuinely surprised them. Maybe stop expecting yourself to be a superhero. (Even superheroes get irritable.)

What are you feeling and why?

"I feel ___ because ___." Then keep going until there's a period at the end of the sentence. This is such an effective exercise to do because it really asks you to get to the root of how you're feeling.

"I feel anxious because I have so much to do… because I'm already behind… because I keep thinking I'm going to mess something up… because honestly I feel like I'm not handling things the way I should be."

"I feel annoyed because everyone keeps asking me for things… because I already have too much on my plate… because I haven't said no to anything… because I don't even feel like I have a choice in my own schedule."

"I feel sad because that didn't go how I wanted… because I thought it would be different this time… because I really wanted it to work… because I think part of me feels like this always happens."

What is working?

Reassessment isn't just about what *isn't* working. Sometimes it's about identifying strengths, supports, and patterns that *are* helping, so that we don't accidentally dismantle something that's helping.

For example, someone might come in feeling overwhelmed and assume nothing is working. But when we slow it down, they realize they've been consistently going to bed earlier, making it to work on time, and reaching out to a friend instead of isolating. These are the wins, and can help to support other issues or areas that *aren't* working so well.

Realign: Coming Back to What Fits

Realignment begins when you notice you've drifted in some way. Perhaps you've reverted to former habits or patterns. Maybe something external has occurred and you're responding to it in a way that feels off.

This is where *why, what,* and *how* become useful. These are short, effective open-ended questions to ask yourself because they invite deeper explanation. *Why* wants to understand causes or reasons. *What* wants information about things, actions, ideas. *How* wants to know about the process

- *Why* did the drift happen?
- *What* changed internally or externally?
- *How* am I prioritizing now — intentionally or not?

Sometimes the answer is obvious. Life got busy. Stress increased. Something unexpected happened. Other times, it's more subtle. You slowly started saying yes to things that don't align. You stopped doing something that was supporting you. You got pulled into old patterns because they were familiar or easier in the moment.

Realignment can look like **adding something back in:**

- Returning to a routine that supported you
- Reconnecting with someone you care about
- Making space for something that brings meaning or purpose

Realignment can look like **removing or reducing something:**

- Saying no
- Setting or revising a boundary
- Doing less of what is draining you or feels misaligned

Realignment doesn't always mean changing your behavior right away. Sometimes it means adjusting how you're thinking or what you're expecting of yourself. For example, if your energy is low and your schedule is full, realignment might sound less like, "I have to keep up," and more like, "I need to be more understanding of myself right now."

At its core, realignment is about bringing your values, goals, and daily choices back into alignment so your life no longer feels like it's pulling in competing directions.

Reactivate: With Compassion

Reactivation doesn't require punishment! Be kind, be compassionate, be gentle with yourself. For some people, that feels really challenging to do. In fact, I've seen progress grind to a halt when I ask someone to view themselves with empathy. It's unfamiliar. Uncomfortable. difficult. And when something feels unfamiliar, the brain often defaults back to what it knows—self-criticism, pressure, or old narratives about failure—because those patterns have been practiced far more often.

Questions that can reinforce reactivation with compassion sound like:

- What would you say to a friend who was in this exact situation?
- If someone who really understood you saw this moment, what would they notice that you're overlooking?
- What would it sound like to respond to yourself without judgment right now?
- What would "kind but honest" sound like if you said it to yourself?
- What would your dog tell you?

(Your dog would have only good things to say, by the way.)

Reactivation is about re-engaging with self-empathy, updated information, and a willingness to keep engaging with the process .

Before You Continue

Remember how we talked about change as an ongoing cycle, rather than something with a finish line? That's the same idea here in *Empowerful*. Rather than leave you with an ending, I want to leave you with a process you can return to because you've already done the hard work.

You took the time to think, reflect, journal, draw, or write poetry. You engaged with this process with curiosity, and hopefully with a willingness to understand yourself more clearly. My hope is that you feel more authentically *you* than you have in a long time. And if there was a time when you felt more like yourself, you now have a way to return to that version of you.

There is no finish line here. There is only a process. If you are here, you have already done the hard work. Now you refine it, revise it, and continue to move forward.

Maybe you tear this page out and put it on your fridge or a vision board.

Maybe you write it somewhere you'll see it.

Or maybe you simply remember three words:

Reassess. Realign. Reactivate.

Pause and Reflect

Take a moment to pause and reflect, without trying to fix or solve anything yet.

- Where in your life have you been treating change like a finish line instead of a practice?
- What has felt hardest about change for you lately—and does it make sense when you consider how long the old pattern has been in place?
- Is there a moment you've labeled as a *setback* that might actually be information or feedback instead?

- What might you need to reassess right now—your expectations, your energy, your environment, or your level of support? Something else?
- If you're feeling off, depleted, or irritable, what might you need to reassess first: energy, expectations, support, or alignment with your values?
- Where might you be trying to change in a system that is pulling you back—and how can you stay grounded in your direction anyway?
- What is already working that you may be overlooking or minimizing?
- And just for perspective: what would someone who genuinely cares about you (or your dog) say about how you're doing right now?

AFTERWORD

We've come to the end of our work together, and I'm genuinely glad you'll be moving forward on your own now.

Early on, I shared that I believe there is a conclusion to effective therapy. I love the moment when a client tells me they don't need to schedule another session, that they want to take some time to navigate life using the tools, insight, and progress they've created. Often, we taper sessions first, spacing them out so real life has room to happen, so challenges arise, and clients can practice using what they've learned outside the therapy room.

Some people break it to me gently, as if they don't want to hurt my feelings. Others arrive excited, relieved, and proud to say, "I think I'm good." Both make me smile.

My hope is that this book has brought real value to the time you've spent with it. Reading, reflecting, experimenting, and engaging in a process that I've seen facilitate meaningful change again and again.

I see my role, with clients and with you, as a facilitator of change. Someone who asks thought-provoking questions, offers reflection, listens carefully, provides empathy, and holds a nonjudgmental space where pieces can come together and the picture can become clearer. The hard work has always been yours.

Some of you may have found value right at the beginning, in the *Assess* phase. Maybe that meant checking in with your body by consulting a primary care provider, or discovering that anxiety had a thyroid-related component, realizing a medication needed adjustment, or learning that you weren't getting enough sleep, sunlight, or (drumroll here…) protein.

Others may have found the most relief in *Align*. Perhaps you revised old narratives, softened harsh beliefs about yourself, or began to see your story with more empathy. Maybe you identified strengths that have carried you through difficult seasons. Strengths you can continue to lean on as you grow and move toward what matters.

And maybe some of you found the greatest value in *Activate*. You felt encouraged, supported, and normalized. Maybe it led to doing something small — or something monumental — which, depending on where you're starting from, can sometimes be the exact same thing. Yes, like brushing your teeth or taking a shower.

Above all, I want to express my gratitude for being part of your process.

This work is humbling. The strength, courage, resilience, tenacity, and determination I've witnessed in clients over the years are a privilege to be part of. This book is dedicated to every single person I've worked with.

Thank you for letting me walk alongside you for a bit.

As you move forward, I hope you carry this with you:

You have the ability to pause, to notice, and to choose differently.

You have the capacity to reassess, realign, and reactivate when life shifts.

You have already begun.

And you don't have to do it perfectly to keep going.